Pelican Books

Style and Civilization | Edited by John Fleming and Hugh Honour

Early Renaissance by Michael Levey

Michael Levey has been interested in the Renaissance since he first read Browning and Pater on hot afternoons at school during the Second World War.

Among his books are several on aspects of eighteenth-century European art, and a biography of Mozart. He is fond of Turkey and is the author of *The World of Ottoman Art*. At present he is Director of the National Gallery. He is married to Brigid Brophy and they have a daughter, Kate.

Early Renaissance, first published in 1967, was awarded the Hawthornden Prize in 1968. Its sequel, *High Renaissance*, appeared in 1975.

Michael Levey

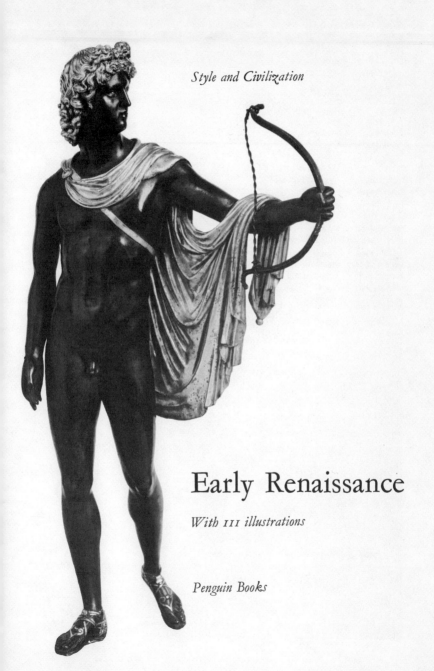

Style and Civilization

Early Renaissance

With 111 illustrations

Penguin Books

Penguin Books Ltd, Harmondsworth, Middlesex, England
Penguin Books, 40 West 23rd Street, New York, New York 10010, U.S.A.
Penguin Books Australia Ltd, Ringwood, Victoria, Australia
Penguin Books Canada Ltd, 2801 John Street, Markham, Ontario, Canada L3R 1B4
Penguin Books (N.Z.) Ltd, 182–190 Wairau Road, Auckland 10, New Zealand

First published 1967
Reprinted 1970, 1977, 1979, 1983, 1987

Designed by Gerald Cinamon
Made and printed in Great Britain by
Richard Clay Ltd, Bungay, Suffolk
Set in Monotype Garamond

HUGH AND JOHN: THEIR BOOK

Contents

Editorial Foreword

The series to which this book belongs is devoted to both the history and the problems of style in European art. It is expository rather than critical. The aim is to discuss each important style in relation to contemporary shifts in emphasis and direction both in the other, non-visual arts and in thought and civilization as a whole. By examining artistic styles in this wider context it is hoped that closer definitions and a deeper understanding of their fundamental character and motivation will be reached.

The series is intended for the general reader but it is written at a level which should interest the specialist as well. Beyond this there has been no attempt at uniformity. Each author has had complete liberty in his mode of treatment and has been free to be as selective as he wished – for selection and compression are inevitable in a series, such as this, whose scope extends beyond the history of art. Not all great artists or great works of art can be mentioned, far less discussed. Nor, more specifically, is it intended to provide anything in the nature of an historical survey, period by period, but rather a discussion of the artistic concepts dominant in each successive period. And, for this purpose, the detailed analysis of a few carefully chosen issues is more revealing than the bird's-eye view.

Early Renaissance

I said that the Renaissance of the fifteenth century was, in many things, great rather by what it designed or aspired to do, than by what it actually achieved.

WALTER PATER

I

What is the Renaissance?

This might seem one of those questions that judges like to put in court to get a laugh; but the answer is not so easy. Everyone has heard of the Renaissance, even though its once superior prestige has dwindled in recent years, challenged by the rising interest in other periods of history and artistic achievement. Indeed, in the excitement of doing justice to them, the Renaissance has sometimes been parcelled out into non-existence. If we explain the Early Renaissance as merely the culmination of medieval trends of thought and the later or High Renaissance merely as a foretaste of the Baroque – then it has virtually ceased to have any positive validity of its own. Of course, this sort of trick may be played on any historical period, showing its indebtedness to the past and its anticipation of the future, and making it entirely an age of transition. And to some extent every age is a transition, just as is every human life; but like each life, it also possesses a character of its own.

Something more complex applies to the elusive, highly fluid history of styles of art. They are convenient umbrellas under which several very distinct and different personalities will often be found sheltering. Even as tolerably coherent a movement as Impressionism – which we should probably treat in a very arbitrary fashion were it something dimly recorded as having happened in the twelfth century – is seen on examination to be made up of artists with quite different, even conflicting, aims. On the one hand, it would be wrong to hasten to assume then that there was no such movement as Impressionism; on the other, it is wrong to turn the Impressionists into an anonymous flock of sheep led by a shepherd called Monet. (No doubt if it had been a twelfth-century movement scholars would have presumed that a scribe's blunder had brought into existence also an artist called Manet.)

Such awkwardnesses apply with particular aptness to any recognition or explanation of the Renaissance. Considered in regard to art alone, the Renaissance is still not a movement or a style comparable to those like Mannerism or Neo-Classicism which provide other titles in this series. It was, to begin with, not strictly an art-historical phenomenon. Many of its finest figures are scholars and great writers with little or no interest in art; they are part of an intellectual tradition which has grown steadily stronger, at least in England, and resulted in philistine blindness being deepest at our oldest universities. Petrarch was friendly with Simone Martini, as we are often proudly told; and Dr Johnson was friendly with Sir Joshua Reynolds, but it would be foolish to accuse Dr Johnson of any interest in the visual arts. The Renaissance was not really the golden age of fine art which it used to be represented as being. Nowadays it is recognized that the apparently commanding role of Lorenzo de' Medici as great patron was partly the result of later Medici propaganda. Though that myth has been demolished, the myth of golden fifteenth-century Florence is still with us. 'Styles of sculpture, painting and architecture had emerged which were to become in the course of time an academic norm lasting almost to our own day' is a recent historian's way of stating it. Before bowing agreement, we should reflect that this statement would have been received with incredulity all over Europe during most of the two centuries between 1600 and 1800. It has silently removed the real claimant, the international standard superbly set up by the seventeenth century. And however highly we may estimate the art of Brunelleschi, Donatello, and Masaccio, we cannot force Bernini, Wren, Poussin, Velazquez, and Rubens, for example, to acknowledge descent from figures in whom they had no interest whatsoever. If one is looking for a century of solid artistic gold – spread throughout Europe, too – then one must turn to the seventeenth century and find one's 'Renaissance' there. And the generating impetus in Italy for that richness comes not from Florence but from Rome and Venice.

Even more than most periods, the Renaissance probably *was* an age of transition. If this is so, it is probably because it wanted to be – at least, it intended to be different from the age that had preceded it. This consciousness is the first sign that separates it and gives it character. It has been left to posterity to label periods Gothic, or Baroque, or Neo-Classical. But the Renaissance virtually called itself by that name, formulating the concept that it had given re-birth to something, had witnessed a renewal of some activities, and was destined to be a restored golden age. In varying degrees the belief runs from Petrarch, who died in 1374, to the art historian and artist Giorgio Vasari who died exactly two hundred years later. It finds its most confident expression in the optimistic letters of Erasmus, written on the eve of the Reformation, which look forward to morality, Christian piety, and 'also a genuine and purer literature' coming to renewed life or greater splendour all over Europe: 'at Rome by Pope Leo, in Spain by the Cardinal of Toledo, in England by Henry VIII, himself not unskilled in letters, and among ourselves by our young King Charles... In France King Francis, who seems as it were born for this object, invites and entices from all countries men that excel in merit and learning.'

All this was in conscious contrast to the iron age of the Goths, those Middle Ages (another term invented by the Renaissance), the barbarous 'Greek' (namely Byzantine) times when art was at its crudest. It does not matter that this was bad history, as wrongly deduced with regard to the past as were Erasmus's hopes for the future. It gave confidence in modern artistic and intellectual achievement, whatever the political situation; it was placing the onus not on God but on man, and thus it had already made some advance into a rational universe. And, of course, although Erasmus might be among those who could not see it, the Reformation was part of a moral movement. Luther was to say of his struggle to comprehend justification by faith: 'I felt myself to be reborn'; he also is part of the Renaissance.

To the idea of superiority over the immediately previous period, a common enough feeling at many periods, the Renaissance added something rather different from any simple notion of progress. It wanted to remain traditional, but it chose the tradition of antiquity rather than Christianity – not at all in conscious opposition but as bringing in an element of truth, nature, philosophy, that medieval Christianity had ignored. Antiquity had become hallowed and literally holy, *sacrosancta vetustas*. Thus the Renaissance looked back to a mythical period of the past – a generalized classical age no more specifically of *one* date than is the scene of Raphael's *School of Athens* – and aspired to be not merely like that but in fact better: by synthesizing antique and modern knowledge there would come the most truthful philosophy, the best literature, the finest works of art. Everything in Italy encouraged this idea; it was, it had to be, a particularly Italian myth because there stood Rome, an imperial capital which had become the Christian capital of the world. The sense of that continuity was no Renaissance discovery; it was a fact never totally lost sight of in the darkest of dark ages and had been most coherently expressed by Dante. A thread of heredity, again expressed patently in Dante, bound Italians to their great past in an emotional way that could not be quite the same for other nations. Rome and antiquity formed a banner which the Renaissance could brandish as it went forward, but both were signs rather than causes. The fully Renaissance achievement of Flemish fifteenth-century painting was not instigated by antiquity or classical scholarship (despite some sprinkled references to Pliny); indeed, that achievement is a clear hint that the impetus came from elsewhere. When the great antiquarian Cyriacus of Ancona wanted to praise a triptych by his contemporary Rogier van der Weyden he could find no better phrase than to say that it appeared not made by the hand of man but by all-creating nature herself, *'ipsa omniparente natura'*.

The Renaissance no more discovered nature than it discovered antiquity, but it made something new of its interest in Nature – justifying the capital letter and eventually bringing it close to challenging Christianity. Although it has long been fashionable to think of Renaissance philosophy almost entirely in terms of Neo-Platonism, the more significant and relevant aspect of it lay in what could be called Neo-Platonic Aristotelianism. This doctrine, with all its complicated permutations in the mouths of different teachers, placed man, rational, mortal man, firmly on the earth. It found a home at the university of Padua and natural sympathies at Venice. The inherent conflict between it and the Church is quite open in the work of one of the most distinguished philosophers, Pietro Pomponazzi (1462–1525), who admitted no miracles, no demons or angels, and who sought an explanation for all phenomena in natural causes: 'All prophecy . . . or the inventions of the arts and sciences, in a word, all the effects observed in this lower world, whatever they be, have a natural cause.' Before the end of the sixteenth century Galileo was to occupy a Chair at the university of Padua and his pursuit of scientific truth, derived at least in method from Aristotelianism, was to bring him into the most famous of all clashes with that Church which presumed to be the guardian of truth. And the typical tendencies of Early Renaissance art to place man in his own environment – itself realized with the maximum science – can be claimed as much more truly inspired by Aristotle than by Plato.

The truth of the human condition, however uncomfortable, was what was nagging at men's minds. Despite what is usually supposed, this climate was not automatically suitable for the flourishing of the arts. They were blooming in an age of (almost) reason and, as was to happen again in the eighteenth century, might find themselves nipped in their more luxuriantly imaginative growths. Botticelli, once thought of as a symbol of the whole Renaissance, is in fact a most untypical figure and one who had probably passed out of fashion well before his death in 1510. In a world of scientific naturalism his art must have looked very 'Gothic' – and it went on seeming so for about three subsequent centuries during which it was almost completely ignored. The Early Renaissance placed more emphasis in art on knowledge than on beauty, and as a result there is a disconcerting vein of naturalism in much of the sculpture and painting which it produced. To our eyes, adapted to expect and enjoy every possible convention and non-convention in art, there is perhaps nothing harder to assimilate than the naturalistic-seeming work of art which is intended not as a joke [1] but as a serious expression of faith in man and in God. It is no accident that the Renaissance has slipped low in the hierarchy of appreciation, because it sometimes seems to lack confidence in *art* as such, to clip imagination's wings in a way not done by the preceding period nor by the style of Mannerism that emerged from it.

By juxtaposing it to its past we can detect something of its quality and aspirations. Against the structure of the Gothic world, the Renaissance takes immediate form. Something of what it was about, and something of the scope of this book, is apparent if a plant study by Leonardo da Vinci [3] is compared with a flower of a different kind, the Golden Rose [2] sent early in the fourteenth century by Pope Clement V to the Prince-Bishop of Bâle. Today this blooms fragilely in a glass case in the Musée de Cluny at Paris; it is one of the very few of these once-common Papal presents to survive. Refined, intricate, exquisitely wrought to a point of almost wilful artificiality – a sapphire at the centre of its corolla of petals – this long-stemmed spray may stand as a representative of the

Gothic style. For all its material beauty, it remains a symbolic object, almost a mystical rose, blessed by the Pope on the one Sunday of rejoicing during Lent, dispatched across Europe as a personal mark of graciousness – usually to sovereigns, and evocative of a united Christendom. It belongs to a climate of myth where the material world, or reality, is only a reflection of a non-material truth: the truth, for Gothic man, of God. A work of art, like all visual beauty in that context, is to be apprehended for its symbolic significance. To take the most famous example, all the treasures accumulated by Abbot Suger at Saint-Denis are explained, and defended, by the theory that they are mere outward expressions of inner reverence and aspiration. They form in effect a stairway of beaten gold and the largest available pearls, that conducts the soul out of this world and into the symbolic gold and pearl of heaven.

By such unearthly standards must Clement V's Golden Rose be judged. When everything constantly symbolized everything else, art was in many ways more free in fantasy, richer and bolder in its effects. Nature existed to be drawn out, twisted, expanded, gilded, and adorned. The ultimate purpose lay in praising God; what art imitated was something no one had ever seen – and the Gothic artist exulted in that freedom not to follow but to invent. This aspect of the pre-Renaissance world was noticed, with no pleasure, by Suger's contemporary St Bernard who spoke of 'so rich and so amazing a variety of forms' to be found carved in cloisters. For what seemed to him an unnatural variety he found the apt phrase '*deformis formositas ac formosa deformitas*' ('deformed beauty and beautiful deformity') which paid tribute to the artist's creative powers, dangerously challenging the Creator's. From Romanesque and Gothic we are led on to Mannerism; St Bernard has unwittingly provided a phrase that would also serve for Bronzino's paintings and the decorations of the Gallery at Fontainebleau. But it has no application to the ideals of at least Early Renaissance art.

When Leonardo drew his plant study, he was urged on by truth, truth to natural observation. Symbolism and the supernatural have nothing to do with it; and though we call the result a work of art it was probably executed as a naturalist's visual note. Even if Leonardo had ever utilized it in one of his paintings, that would not have altered its original purpose. Art itself is for him a matter not of outward splendour – solid

1. Man Looking out of a Window. Bourges, Hôtel de Jacques Cœur

2. Golden Rose

3. Plant Study. Leonardo da Vinci

gold and jewels – but of intellectual manifestation. Its splendours are cerebral ones. And with Leonardo art was constantly being replaced by the sheer wish to know. 'I set myself diligently to consider the source of its life', he recorded when he was experimenting with the intake of moisture by a gourd, and the effect on it of dew. We are back from heaven to earth. It would be no answer for Leonardo to tell him that God is its source of life. He is behaving like an Aristotelian – certainly no Florentine was ever less a Platonist – and is indeed in the direct tradition of Aristotle's pursuit of the natural sciences. The method is more important than the results. Leonardo, little interested in classical scholarship or antiquity (a supreme example of how inessential this was to Renaissance activity), is concerned to establish truth by question and experiment, not through tradition and accepted beliefs.

Leonardo may seem an extreme case of scientific scepticism, and not every Renaissance artist wished to challenge and experiment – even supposing they all had possessed adequate intellectual powers. But in every field there was attempted a new grasp on the fact of Man and a wish to set him on his feet in the world without too much indebtedness to God. Where the Middle Ages had certainly admired the classics, they had also enlisted them as part of the Christian order – or made them subjects of myth. Virgil's Fourth Eclogue entitled him to an honorary position of prophet *manqué* in the Christian scheme; less seriously, he turns up throughout medieval poems as a great magician. In neither manifestation can he be thought of as an historical person who had actually existed. The past of antiquity was a misty, magical scene until Petrarch wrote *Letters to the Ancient Dead* which make actual not only the gulf of time but the existence of the addressees: they lived once as much as the person now writing to them.

The shift from medieval to Renaissance concepts in history has been pointed out by Federico Chabod in contrasting Dante's contemporary, and perhaps source, Giovanni Villani with Machiavelli. Villani's historical chronicle was to be utilized by Machiavelli when writing his own history of Florence, but he picked out the facts without taking any of the moralizing religious framework with which Villani liked to surround them. Machiavelli's history is a terse narrative of events as they may be supposed to have happened. Villani sees disasters as punishment for sins; his narrative is interrupted by exhortations to his fellow-Florentines to correct their errors and become pleasing to the most high God. Machiavelli's world is a political one activated by men's wills not by a supernatural will above.

A vivid literary shift of exactly the same kind is seen in comparing Shakespeare's *Troilus and Cressida* with Chaucer's poem on the same theme – the more dramatic because for most of its length Chaucer's wonderful poem preserves a completely non-Christian tone. It opens with a classical invocation and speaks of its author as servant of Love's servants, begging them to pray for those lovers who suffer a fate like Troilus. But it ends with an almost shocking palinode in which Chaucer turns on his hero, the whole false pagan structure, and all worldly vanity. It is Christ and his love on which we must ponder: 'What nedeth feyned loves for to seke?' The book which was to be sent to 'kis the steppes' where had

trodden 'Virgile, Ouyde, Omer, Lucan and Stace' finishes
with a solemn invocation to the Trinity and the Virgin. As for
the bitter, disenchanted realism of Shakespeare's play, non-
Christian and non-classical, it might indeed have come from
the pen of a political historian like Machiavelli with its con-
temptuous explanatory prologue of what we shall see: 'Now
good or bad, 'tis but the chance of war.'

In art a shift away from medieval thought is early expressed
in the work of the Florentine painter, goldsmith, sculptor,
and probably architect too, Lorenzo Ghiberti – most patently
in his work as a writer. Ghiberti (1378–1455) was one of the
first to provide anything resembling art history and the first
artist to provide an autobiography, as well as a vivid self-
portrait [4]. His three *Commentarii* run from an account of

4. *Self-Portrait.* Ghiberti

ancient art, derived from classical sources like Pliny, to the story of how he won the competition to design the bronze doors of the Baptistery at Florence. Long before Cellini, Ghiberti exuded what at that time seems a new boastfulness in the individuality of his achievement, in the fact of everything being his own work. He is not learned but confident. He writes in the vernacular, Italian. Posterity shall know about Ghiberti, and not merely through his artistic works. There is an exuberant egotism about his claims which makes almost charming the iteration of the importance of being Ghiberti: *his* artistic victories, *his* universally recognized genius, *his* contributions to the embellishment of Florence ('Few things were made in our country that were not designed and planned by me'). It is hard not to cheer the old man writing it all down; and it is even harder to deny the truth of most of it.

Along with the fresh emphasis on the artist's personal power to create, there goes also a new attitude to the achievements of antiquity. The idea of renaissance in the arts which Vasari was putting forward a century or so later was already outlined by Ghiberti. There is a hint of resentment in his account of the triumph of Christianity which interrupted the progress of the arts; that latent aspiration for a world moral rather than religious makes Ghiberti temperamentally Renaissance rather than Gothic. Under Constantine, he relates, the Christian faith was victorious; idolatry was persecuted, and as a result all the noble antique statues were destroyed, and all the rules of art. Painting and sculpture ceased to exist – to be revived only in the time of Giotto, a Florentine of course, who invented or discovered many methods 'which had been buried for about six hundred years'. Ghiberti tells the same story of sculpture, in Italy with the Pisano, and more unexpectedly in Germany where there flourished at Cologne a mysterious Master Gusmin 'the equal of the ancient Greek sculptors'. We have no knowledge of this artist or his work, but Ghiberti's text breathes respect for a great teacher who ended up as a hermit of great sanctity; and it serves as a reminder which is badly needed that the Renaissance was never a purely Italian phenomenon, even in Italian eyes.

The metaphor of burial and excavation becomes accomplished fact in the emergence from the earth of antique sculpture. Once again, this is not in itself a particularly Renaissance phenomenon; it is the attitude to it which changes, and which is documented by Ghiberti. He speaks of an

antique statue dug up at Siena, drawn by Ambrogio Lorenzetti (therefore presumably at some time in the first half of
the fourteenth century) and placed on the fountain in the
main piazza. Ghiberti knew it only in Lorenzetti's drawing,
because during an early war between Siena and Florence it
had been taken down and buried by the Sienese in Florentine
territory. A citizen of Siena had persuaded his countrymen
that their disasters arose through God's anger; idolatry was
being punished and their troubles would end only when the
statue had been taken away from Sienese territory. The idea
of passing on the curse by reburying the statue in Florentine
land was undoubtedly ingenious, and shows how much taboo
was then attached to the whole concept of an antique object.
In Ghiberti's own day it was already a story of superstition.
He had no dreadful disasters to relate in connexion with the
activities of the Florentine collector Niccolo Niccoli (died
1427), who assembled Latin and Greek manuscripts and
objects – among them a marvellous antique chalcedony
intaglio: 'the most perfect thing I ever saw', Ghiberti writes.
It was becoming obvious that God did not smite down
citizens who admired such things. Ghiberti's interest is
purely artistic. He did not understand the iconography of the
gem, and admired it because it was vividly natural. And
while it is true that many intellectual and artistic aims were
directed towards a synthesis of antiquity and Christianity,
this movement was really the aspiration towards a truer and
more natural world-picture in which eventually both
Christianity and antiquity would have diminished in importance. The whole mixture of experience was being shaken up;
the final dose was stiffer than the Renaissance could have
guessed, and yet it had already stumbled on the possibility that
we are alone in the universe.

Whether alone or not, man himself is the Renaissance
preoccupation. When definitions fail we can turn to works of
art and see in them best of all the quintessence of this concern.
Certain long-famous, much admired works state the theme
and partly answer the question posed by this introduction:
they give us man as he stands forth early in the fifteenth
century, with fresh awareness rather than fresh confidence,
broken away from the past and placed in a new relationship
to his environment. Aspects of that environment require
chapters of study in themselves; it evolves and changes, growing more sophisticated. But the *dramatis persona* himself,

5. *St George.*
Donatello

whether as saint or as ordinary human being, to be seen in Southern and Northern Europe, will hardly be found more memorably created than by Donatello and Jan van Eyck – active contemporaneously for some twenty years up to van Eyck's death in 1441.

Donatello's marble *St George* [5] held its proud aesthetic position throughout the Renaissance, as warmly admired in the sixteenth as in the fifteenth century. The sculptor himself

6. *The Marriage of Giovanni* (?) *Arnolfini and Giovanna Cenami* (?). Jan van Eyck

was the sole figure who could suitably be paragoned with Michelangelo; Vasari mentioned approvingly the epigram contrived by his friend Don Vincenzo Borghini, the Prior of S. Marco, which neatly implied Donatello's inspiration of Michelangelo or alternatively that Michelangelo first inspired Donatello: '*Aut Donatus Bonarrotum exprimit et refert, aut Bonarrotus Donatum.*' During his own lifetime Donatello's status in Florence had been such that Cosimo de' Medici chose that they should be buried close together, and Donatello's funeral was probably the most public and splendid given to any Florentine artist until the obsequies for Michelangelo almost a century later. What Donatello had achieved was in general expressed in the epitaphs: he had put nature into marble, giving inanimate blocks life, sense, and movement. In no other work had he more patently done so than in the *St George* whose vivacity and alertness were consistently praised.

Yet Donatello's 'nature' in this statue was really greater than any of the praise made explicit. A psychological realism was there combined with three-dimensional realism: the same truth to the emotions that made of his *Virgin Annunciate* [74] a woman timid, humble, and grateful. There is a conflict between the first impression of static confidence in St George's pose and one's gradual awareness of a tendency to movement, an almost uneasy shifting of the feet, which combines with the more than uneasy expression of the face. It is not defiance which the Saint proclaims, and he can hardly be supposed to be guarding anything, because his shield is at rest. Even if originally he held a lance in his right hand and wore a helmet, there must still have been some sense of unprotectedness in him: the worried, puzzled air of someone who scents danger without being able to account for it [7]. His heroism – and the figure's impact is heroic – is that of nervous energy keyed up but uncertain of how long it can sustain this tension. Thus cased within a clinging armoured carapace of leather and metal (itself a *tour de force* of rendering in marble and a sharp reminder that the armourers' guild, the Corazzi, commissioned the statue) is a man more than a saint. He was on man's level too, quite literally, for one of the remarkable things about the niches at Or San Michele is their comparative closeness to the ground, making it easy for the spectator to establish contact with the figures in them. While the relief under the statue shows the Saint's physical prowess in overcoming the

7. Head of *St George* (detail of 5)

dragon, the statue itself enshrines spiritual crisis. Not accidentally – for Donatello was a master of calculating effects *in situ* – it by no means fills the niche which echoes emptily over it, separating the small, almost ineffectual, blessing God the Father carved above from the prominent lonely Saint below, more dependent on his own human capacities than on divine aid.

With this inner naturalness and truth is allied virtuosity of handling – a virtuosity which on the surface would have been yet more striking before the statue had so long been exposed to weathering. The individuality of the face, the creasing of the eyebrows where they meet the nose, the delicately wrinkled forehead, might have been created by a Gothic observer, but hardly the fusion of such details into the harmoniously proportioned, sculptural whole – relation of head to body – and the sense of a body itself under the armour. The Renaissance idea of life in the stone, or rather the stone brought to life and qualities of *vivacità* and *prontezza* communicating outwards to make art more living than ordinary existence, is perfectly expressed by virtuosity and a command which remain free of rhetoric. The statue lives so effectively because it remains statuesque; it hints at movement but expresses this in potentiality rather than as fact. No gesture astonishes or stops the spectator; and its final power comes not from its existence in a dimension beyond our own but from seeming to be so like ourselves.

Only against Jan van Eyck's yet plainer humanity does it seem ideal. His 'nature' equally astonished the fifteenth century by its realism and its superb technical competence. The Genoese humanist, Bartolomeo Fazio, writing about 1455–6 at the Naples court of Alfonso of Aragon, included van Eyck's biography among his lives of famous men, *de Viris Illustribus*, and stated his commanding place as '*pictorum princeps*' of the century. Van Eyck's knowledge was what was recognized. His '*art et science*' were unique too in the eyes of his patron Philip of Burgundy who, if he did not express a wish to have the artist buried near him, at least honoured him highly and stood sponsor at the christening of van Eyck's child. Whereas Donatello might easily be connected with antique achievements, it was less easy to see how Jan van Eyck could be supposed indebted to the classical past. Lip-service of a sort was paid by Fazio who claimed he had learnt from reading Pliny, but the results were entirely non-classical.

It is first as a triumph of modern science that one can see *The Marriage of Giovanni* (?) *Arnolfini and Giovanna Cenami* (?) [6] where ordinary man, and woman, are completely held in a cube of their environment: a geometrical theorem which has passed out of science into art through van Eyck's technique. It is as if a mirror were held up to nature; and by a happy chance one of the van Eyck paintings mentioned by Fazio did contain a marvellous rendering of a mirror which reflected what one might see in an actual mirror. In another picture, known personally to him, there was painted a ray of sunshine which might be mistaken for real sunlight. And it is easy to conceive the terms in which Fazio would have praised the Arnolfini group had he known of it.

The picture would have been less remarkable, in Fazio's eyes, for what it shows than for how it shows it. It is almost a magical optical trick, made possible by an empirical grasp of perspective, that gives the effect of peering into a room: a room which, owing to the mirror painted in it, is able to include part of the wall and doorway behind the actual spectator. And all this is achieved on the flat surface of a piece of wood in area hardly more than five square feet. The picture thus becomes an object half-way between peep-show and mirror. Early Renaissance fascination with mirrors is attested almost contemporaneously by Brunelleschi's device whereby one looked through a hole in the back of a painting by him and saw his composition reflected in a mirror behind; and the practice of consulting a mirror to check the effect of a painting is recommended to artists by Alberti.

Van Eyck's is the most illusionistic device of all because it is achieved entirely in paint. And the medium of oil-paint covered by a varnish is itself part of the magical technical skill which Italy admired: it was a 'secret' comparable to the secret process of making glass mirrors – much more esteemed than merely metal ones because, as Vincent of Beauvais had recorded in the thirteenth century, '*vitrum propter transparentiam melius recipit radios*' ('Because of its transparency, glass best transmits rays'). It is through, as it were, the glass of the varnish that rays of light illuminate the bedroom where the Arnolfini stand. Although the sunlight effect praised by Fazio is absent, there is, in addition to the painted mirror on the back wall, the half-open window of glowing glass with foliage and sky visible beyond – a further capturing of atmospheric effect, for the sky is not flat blue, nor even decorated with cloud, but liquid, nearly colourless, a sheer radiance which seems the very element of air. Just as much as had Donatello, Jan van Eyck captures *vivacità*. He is conscious of the dignity of being human; and a marvellous allegory of life as he may have conceived it is contained in the mirror which at its centre reflects the Arnolfini and frames them round with scenes of Christ's Passion.

Donatello's *St George* was a public work of art, a guild commission in would-be democratic Florence, destined for a church façade, and intended primarily to be a religious object. Hints of the boy David combine in it with hints of the Archangel Michael: promise of victory after effort is adumbrated: the human form is animated by the power of God. As such it might have appeared on the façade of any Gothic cathedral. But Donatello expresses the religious meaning in a new way: saintliness is conveyed by a perfection of the body and by a harmony of proportions which consciously recall the Greek ideal of the athlete and the warrior. The enemy St George faces is not made visible – indeed, nothing is sculpted that could not be seen in ordinary life; hence the result is a natural vision, easily assimilated and comprehended, and yet astonishing. What is intensified are the physical and mental qualities of any man: sharpened to a keener tension, moulded to make a prouder pose, all on a scale somewhat larger than life but recognizably related to life. It is a solid, three-dimensional marble man who stands in the shallow niche – from which he is ready to move, if necessary. And one must try to recover an almost naïve response to this lifelike image, whose vivid reality was enhanced at the time of its execution by the bronze accoutrements of sword or lance, helmet or wreath. It was not the saintliness expressed by the statue that the Renaissance praised; it told of no miracles wrought by it, because the *St George* was itself a miracle and Donatello the miracle-worker. Perhaps no work of art since antiquity had seemed so completely natural – to the point where one might easily ignore its religious origin – and so completely ideal.

The purpose behind van Eyck's painting is private: a private commission, intended to have private significance (probably never meant to be seen outside the sitters' family), it is the pictorial version of a diary, recording an event and also the environment which concerned the Arnolfini. It is *their* room and *their* dog and *their* shoes (carefully differentiated, hers of scarlet leather and his of wood), which are painted, as well as themselves. A solemn, even religious moment is depicted; marriage is a sacrament. But even the human witnesses have dwindled to minute figures just glimpsed in the mirror. Ordinary genre detail absorbs religious significance. Once again, nothing is recorded that could not have been seen by anyone present. The only supernatural clue is the candle burning by daylight in the chandelier; that may be odd but is hardly an obtrusive symbol. Van Eyck's scale is much smaller than life, and his vision more magically microscopic. His wintry-faced people are not inspiring, nor harmoniously proportioned; far from expressing, they conceal emotion, and perhaps pride themselves on such dignified concealment. Psychologically, the picture is slack where Donatello's statue was keen (in that, it is Rogier van der Weyden's work [8] which is comparable to Donatello's).

Yet both picture and statue are impregnated with a new sense of what it is like to be alive. This is not in any way set up in opposition to religion – in fact, it is positively set within the Christian framework in both instances – but does encourage the spectator's interest in his own reactions, both mental and physical. In both works a special knowledge is enshrined: knowledge not only of what the hand can accomplish and the eye can see, but self-knowledge. Art has not gone out on an exotic quest to search for a golden rose but for the simple, yet elusive flower of truth. When we look at these two works of art we are meant to refer back to our own experience, and thus confirm their utter truthfulness. That they are so true is what makes them astonishing: experience has passed from being a subjective state of mind into being crystallized in marble and paint. It is the fact of their own ordinariness – their naturalness – that must have astonished the first spectators. The Arnolfini's room is so like a real – and incidentally quite plain – room; they themselves are not princely but ordinary bourgeois. They suggest the rise of a new class, merchant-banker princes (instead of those of royal blood) and it is fitting that they should have lived in mercantile Bruges. St George is like a real, quite plainly dressed, soldier. Those people who first looked at them, having referred back and found them amazingly true, must have been tempted to reverse the process: to examine their own minds to see if they contained other aspects of human experience which might find expression in art. A fresh relationship had certainly been established between what art expresses and what a human being perceives and feels. It is this dialogue of humanity that is carried on with such increasing eloquence by the Renaissance artist; and fresh examination of experience in general is perhaps the characteristic of all Renaissance activity.

8. *Philippe de Croy*. Rogier van der Weyden

2

'Men of Renown'

It was a marble head of Pericles which prompted Pliny to say that the art of sculpture 'has made men of renown yet more renowned'. That idealized and yet clearly characterized head, surviving in several Roman copies, crystallizes the myth not only of Pericles but of Periclean Athens. City and man are blended, as are military strength and civic wisdom: under the upraised helmet are the features of the statesman. It is a synthesis of *virtù* of the type that was to make a tremendous· appeal in the Renaissance, and its dignified device of avoiding too much commonplace fact was praised by Alberti. If sculpture can do so much to enhance a really renowned man, its power is even greater to launch into immortality the obscure – not often as heroically as in Michelangelo's Medici Chapel, where art and idealization have outwitted history and made renowned the unremarkable Giuliano, Duc de Nemours, and Lorenzo, Duke of Urbino. A double immortality lies in the power of all such art; the artist has his personal share in the renown. Cresilas is remembered only for having been the sculptor of the original head of Pericles. But though the later Renaissance artist might sometimes respectfully speak of going down to posterity on the hem of his patron's garment, his increasing belief was the reverse: 'So long as men can breathe or eyes can see, So long lives this, and this gives life to thee.' Equal pride is apparent behind Ronsard's line: '*Ronsard me célébroit du temps que j'estois belle.*' Perhaps no modern poet before Ronsard had felt so much confidence in the power of his art and his own poetic immortality; it is with full Renaissance boldness, fortified by careful study of Latin and Greek poetry (and a corresponding scorn for earlier French poetry) that he could proclaim: '*vous êtes mes sujets, je suis seul votre roi.*' And not only the ordinary public but royalty too agreed with him. All the more impressive is his praise of a brother-artist, Clouet: '*honneur de nostre France*'.

Along with its discovery of the laws of visual perspective, the Renaissance was discovering the perspective of history.

Its realization of being different from the period preceding it gave it in effect a vantage-point from which it could survey the past, and made it sharply aware of the value of leaving monuments – literary and artistic – for posterity. How man actually lived and actually looked had, of course, always been of interest to mankind. There had been medieval chroniclers, often with a keen eye for effective detail. Vivid detail rather than broad grasp is exactly what characterizes the history both of Matthew Paris and Froissart. It is not only that increasing literacy and awareness were to mean more sophisticated concepts of history – though sometimes a duller, less minutely observed history. The two closely interwoven strata of feudal State and Church which had supplied the chief subject and protagonists for history were breaking up. 'Men of renown' did not mean only great rulers, churchmen or warriors but, as Fazio shows, could be stretched to include painters. Writers of history themselves need have no claim to learning as such; sheer knowledge of what he wrote about, combined with a realization of history's power to preserve fame, impelled the fifteenth-century Florentine bookseller Vespasiano da Bisticci to set down, in Italian, biographies of famous men he had known. This straightforward record-like role is what Dürer singles out as painting's second task: to preserve the appearance of men after their deaths. Alberti had more eloquently said much the same. Vespasiano da Bisticci's shrewd standards are those of humanity and reality. History makes the lives of famous people of the past 'as real to us as if they had lived today'. And the people of the past who move him most are Lycurgus, Scipio, Cato: upright, ideal but true figures, recorded by their own historians, who cast inspiring shadows over the present. After a very skimpy sketch of the murky Florentine past, Vespasiano finds himself full in the renascent brilliance of his own period: 'The present age has produced many distinguished men in all the faculties. . . . In this age all the seven liberal arts have been fruitful in men of distinction. . . .' Such tones go some way to justifying the belief that the Renaissance did express fresh confidence in man's abilities – and they show that fame is not the prerogative of a prince.

Even where the Renaissance prince planned to have himself immortalized by art, it was not always his fame as such which was emphasized. Arrogant splendour and what might almost be called the fantasy of fame are better exemplified in the fourteenth-century Scaligeri tombs at Verona than in the quietly domestic Gonzaga frescoes by Mantegna at Mantua. Pride of life and intense reaction to death are more typical of Gothic man, or post-Renaissance man seen in a welter of jewels and blood by, for instance, Webster. The extreme quality of these expressions contrasts with all Renaissance aspiration towards harmony: harmony of man first in relation to other men, and then in the cosmic framework of nature and God. Secure in fame, man strives towards eternity.

In all this, history plays its part. Knowledge of the past is brought in to help the present, and when Vespasiano included a woman's life among his biographies he specifically explained it was to serve as an example to 'women today'. In fact, his choice – Alessandra de' Bardi – was a fifteenth-century Florentine, distinguished not by renown or fame in the usual sense but by piety and courage. Looking back into antiquity, Vespasiano compares her to Portia, the wife of Brutus; but she is also seen as deeply religious, charitable, and full of 'modern' human virtues. And it is this new emphasis – on the humane as well as the merely human – that distinguishes these lives. Vespasiano praises knowledge because it is useful; literacy illuminates the world and what makes a man great is less rank than greatness of soul and mind. As for Vespasiano himself – as he announces in, for example, his life of King Alfonso of Naples – he is concerned to write only the real truth ('*la propria verità*'). The fact that he did not always succeed does not militate against his aim. Although the *Lives* are naturally conceived within a completely Christian setting, the final effect is to emphasize character in terms of active virtue, and literacy as among the very highest of virtues. The *Lives* are divided into categories of popes and rulers, cardinals, statesmen, scholars; and the largest category of all is that of scholars.

It is in terms of '*la propria verità*', without emphasis on rank or renown, that Mantegna sets out to record in paint the Gonzaga court in Mantua. Just as Vespasiano da Bisticci puts down his own recollections (scrupulously accounting for what he did not personally witness) so Mantegna underlines the witness quality of these frescoes by signing them as executed to honour the Marchese Ludovico Gonzaga by *his* Andrea Mantegna, himself their instigator and artist.

At the farthest interior of the Palace the Gonzaga family and their friends assemble on the walls as if in life. They meet

9. *Marchese Gonzaga Welcoming his Son Cardinal Francesco*. Andrea Mantegna

10. *The Gonzaga Court*. Andrea Mantegna

Cardinal Francesco newly returned from Rome [9] – not with some gorgeous triumphal procession in the 'Renaissance' style of Baron Corvo, but almost casually and with a dignified intimacy and unselfconsciousness exemplified by the Cardinal holding hands with his younger brother who in turn has his fingers grasped by the youngest boy of all. A yet greater mood of relaxation is apparent in the fresco of the assembled court [10], where the Marchese turns away to speak to a secretary and a Gonzaga girl leans over her mother's lap, just about to take a bite from an apple. This art might almost have been drawn in equal parts from Jan van Eyck and Donatello; it substitutes for van Eyck's cubes of physical environment a social environment filled by people rather than objects.

Everyone has his place in this world, is brought into relationship, or at least proximity, with other human beings; there is even a place for the noble dog, crouched under the Marchese's chair. There is no narrative, no particular incident depicted, no overt religious reference – even the return of the newly-made Cardinal in the other fresco being treated more in terms of a graduation day ceremony. It is the continuity of life, not some arrested moment of it, that is stressed. Time is passing; the grouped courtiers will shift position; the Marchese turn back, his daughter eat her apple; the interlocked brothers will set off for home. So much is postulated, but nothing will really change. Mantegna has sliced out of time this aspect of life at the Gonzaga court in Mantua in the fifteenth century; the frescoes are overpoweringly full of his own knowledge of the personalities presented here so vividly and quite unflatteringly. They are not being put on public display, are not stirring us to admire their heroism or their beauty, or their virtue – only their vitality. No claim is made for these people except that they are human and alive; thence comes their dignity. It is because they are real that they are painted – and the whole depiction would be pointless did they not exist. Having no power to create an image by itself, a mirror can reflect only when something is present. Of course Mantegna's art is much more than an automatic reflection; but it sets up a challenge to reality and hints at the infinity of mirror facing mirror. Alberti praised the divine power of painting that can make the absent present; Mantegna goes one step further, defying anyone in the presence of the Gonzaga to tell which is the real and which the painted family.

When Vasari was writing about Mantegna and his period he looked back over nearly a century and distinguished it as a time when 'men of genius were busily engaged in investigating and imitating the truths of Nature'. Ludovico Gonzaga was not the only prince to be mirrored as a human being rather than ruler, caught in the diurnal aspect of ordinary domestic life, and to have this mirror image placed before him in privacy. In the studiolo of the palace at Urbino [11],

11. The Studiolo of Federigo da Montefeltro. Urbino, Palazzo Ducale

the great hero of Vespasiano da Bisticci's *Lives*, Federigo da Montefeltro was shown not only in the Periclean duality of warrior–statesman but with the additional aspect of scholar [12]; there he was depicted '*al naturale*' and there lacked nothing except '*lo spirito*'. Nor was the universal concept of him a false one. Federigo da Montefeltro is one of the few Renaissance princes who really was a brilliant soldier, a clever, prudent ruler, and a liberal patron of the arts. All those aspects of his career are to be found in Vespasiano's life of him; but on none is greater emphasis laid than on his combination of these abilities with what can only be called accessible humanity. Not even his marvellous library (which Vespasiano

12. *Federigo da Montefeltro and his Son.* Pedro Berruguete (?)

had collected for him), with its books on music, painting, medicine – not to mention the Fathers of the Church, and Homer, Pindar, Menander – could rival that remarkable aspect which occurs on page after page of Vespasiano's recital: '*tanta umanità . . . sua inaudita umanità . . . con tutti*'. He told Vespasiano once how necessary it was for anyone ruling a kingdom '*essere umano*'. Because, he said, it was the first thing expected of a ruler. And the *Life* is full of stories of his humane actions, in which he constantly mingled with his subjects in the market-place, on his estates, or in his palace.

That palace is his monument, secular not religious, and less aggressively personal than Sigismondo Malatesta's rather earlier temple at Rimini. Designed about the middle of the fifteenth century by Luciano Laurana, it still seemed a beautiful building to the succeeding century – according to many the most beautiful palace in all Italy, said Castiglione, who made it the setting for *Il Cortigiano*. Vasari found it as fine and well constructed as any palace built up to his own period. It appeared to Castiglione not so much a palace as a city in the form of a palace. Huge and yet graceful, it still retains its sense of being inhabited, and furnished, despite the many empty rooms. Much bigger than the town palaces of Florence, it avoids being merely a fortress. It impresses by harmony rather than strength. The first historian to describe it, the sixteenth-century author Baldi, emphasizes its literal lucidity of plan, with every room beautifully lit thanks to the disposition of the courtyards, and its ease of arrangement owing to the placing of the different staircases. Elsewhere staircases could themselves become works of art – seldom with more marvellously planned spatial effects than those achieved at Venice by Coducci [13], a superb reminder that intellect and artistic control were not the prerogative of Tuscany.

From the first, the palace at Urbino was intended to be habitable, and the 'magnificence' of the prince partly consisted in his practicality (no ceilings of wood, Baldi mentions, because of the danger of fire). The entrance gateways are almost casually graceful, hardly more imposing than doorways into rooms – in strong contrast to the elaborate Triumphal Arch begun earlier in the century by Alfonso of Aragon as the entrance to his Castle at Naples [14, 15], where Virtues and Saints, and the King himself sculpted in a Roman processional frieze, put a bold architectural front on Alfonso's military achievements.

13. Staircase. Mauro Coducci. Venice, Scuola Grande di S. Giovanni Evangelista

14. Triumphal Arch of King Alfonso of Aragon. Naples, Castelnuovo

15. Triumphal Arch (detail of 14)

At Urbino Federigo da Montelfeltro is very much present but unassertively. Indeed, his presence is hinted everywhere in his own palace, in arms, devices and inscriptions, on the doorways [16], the chimneys [17], the windows – always entwined in or made part of the scheme of decoration. One

16. Main Doorway of the Sala della Iole. Urbino, Palazzo Ducale

18. A Window. Attributed to Giovanni Antonio Amadeo. Pavia, Certosa

may compare the interior decoration of Jacques Cœur's house at Bourges, with its running, punning device: '*A vaillans cœurs rien impossible.*' There Cœur himself appears in stone, but in the somewhat later palace at Urbino, Federigo's image is not carved. The emblems of war that frame a doorway are wrought into a decorative frieze that hardly differs from the unallusive, purely ornamental band above them of crisply curling acanthus leaves, rosettes, and springing stiff ears of corn. Always amid tendrils of lightly sculpted vine and carved among the capitals is to be found the Garter motto or the Montefeltro eagle or Federigo's initials, followed by '*Dux*' after he had been created Duke of Urbino by Pope Sixtus IV. Yet all is scrupulously controlled. A palace doorway at Urbino rebukes the excesses of the Lombard Renaissance [18], in which function is smothered by ornament. Laurana's melodiously graceful, arcaded courtyard [19] bears on two levels an inscription as virtually its sole ornament, at once discreet and yet arresting: setting out all Federigo's titles to military glory but stating finally that his victories were

19. Courtyard of the Palazzo Ducale, Urbino.
Attributed to Luciano Laurana

equalled and adorned by his peacetime virtues of justice, clemency, liberality, and religion.

It is to this double ideal that Laurana's palace is constructed; its virtue of graceful habitation as approached from within

Urbino is equalled by its proudly defiant aspect when seen from outside the city, with its two slender-pointed towers flanking a steep façade – dramatic contrast in vertical setting and appearance to the horizontal lines of its town face. The same double ideal was inevitably enshrined in the portrait of Federigo which hung in his own studiolo [11, 12]. In the whole scheme of decoration there was something also of the spatial illusionism with which Mantegna played at Mantua: in painted niches the Liberal Arts sat and were accompanied by actual figures from the Urbino court; inlaid panels of wood simulate half-open cupboards with shelves of books and instruments, and even reveal a pet squirrel. Unassumingly yet very much *there*, the fully-armed Federigo was shown, engaged in reading a book. Everything in this painting speaks of accomplishment; the sitter has nothing left to do but seek knowledge. No pictures were painted of his victories; only of him kneeling in prayer before the Madonna, or listening to a humanist scholar, or – as in the studiolo depiction – of himself as the scholar. This portrait forms a concise biography, much more consciously a history of life than anything Mantegna had depicted. Each object has its meaning for Federigo, beginning with his heir, sickly and pale, a princely child encased in heavy, tremendously jewelled robes, grasping a sceptre – artistic brother almost to the royal children painted by Velazquez – who seeks the support of his father's knee. The State and succession is guaranteed, but Federigo remains armoured. His international diplomacy is conveyed by the Order of the Garter from England, the pearl-encrusted mitre from Persia; dressed as *gonfaloniere* of the Church, he sits in a plain cell-like room, absorbed in the book so eagerly grasped in his forceful, clumsy, arthritic hands – a detail scrupulously recorded, with the same attention to *verità* that characterizes the rest of the picture.

Better than words the new realistic art can sum up the personality of a man, conveying not only his renown but his *vivacità*. In the public rooms of the palace Federigo appeared only allusively; but in private works of art, whether straightforward portraits or religious pictures, he wished to see reflected his own image: that memorable profile, made the more memorable by an accident which caused him always to be shown thus and facing left, which looks tough, shrewd, and sensitive. He was to be shown naturally; '*essere umano*' might have been his motto for the likenesses he comissioned, which never lay emphasis on rank or splendour, and which place the ruler rather in the context of learning or piety. It is unobtrusively that Federigo kneels with his son in the background of Francesco di Giorgio's bronze relief of the Deposition, a quiet figure amid the whirling grieving women.

Under the eye of eternity, juxtaposed to the Virgin or Christ, man had no longer any need to shrink to the proportions of medieval minuteness, expressive of humility. His emergence may be symbolized by Federigo da Montefeltro, but it was apparent everywhere; the motto of Jacques Cœur sounds a new note of high ambition. The evolution of the diptych that combined portrait and personal vision shows man elbowing his way into his half of the object, culminating in Fouquet's Estienne Chevalier diptych where patron and patron saint occupy a marvellous receding tunnel of real spaciousness [20] – the more marked in comparison with the

20. *Estienne Chevalier and St Stephen.* Jean Fouquet

crowded yet flat Virgin and Child panel. There is little change of basic concept between Fouquet's *Virgin and Child* and the theme as treated in the International Gothic style of the Wilton Diptych. But between the profile portrait of Richard II, with his patron saints, and Estienne Chevalier with St Stephen there is a contrast which goes beyond technique. It is not only a matter of the setting, nor even the forceful three-quarter-face presentation of Chevalier. St Stephen is perhaps the real triumph of humanity in the diptych, a powerfully realized portrait 'double' of the donor.

All the forms are economically concentrated to present an uncluttered, intense reality, of geometrical precision but sculptural weight. The saint holds his book tight against his body, as if to make it organically part of him; it serves too as support for the single stone of his martyrdom, a jagged piece of heavy quartz, as individual and actual as the strongly modelled features of the saint's face. Such objects must find a fully three-dimensional world in which to exist, and Fouquet devised a right-angle section of marble-sheeted wall and floor, geometrically patterned and steeply inclined, which provides a perfect mineral setting of polished hardness. A church, perhaps, yet with the air of a temple, it is richly severe, somehow lacking any god except Chevalier himself, whose name is indeed prominently incised on the first pillar. It would hardly be going too far to see here, in one of the very last of such diptychs, a reversal of all the format's original values: the Virgin and Child being present now in honour of Estienne Chevalier. The old tradition that the Virgin is Agnès Sorel, the French king's mistress but loved also by Chevalier, the Royal Treasurer, may be no more than part of a disturbing ambiguity felt to be exuded by the whole diptych. This can have been only the more patent when it was in its original frame of blue velvet, with 'E's embroidered in pearls linked by embroidered gold and silver love-knots. What Chevalier and his painter wanted to express could hardly any longer be done in the restricted, old-fashioned format. The accident of the two halves now being separated, divided between Berlin and Antwerp, is almost symbolic; and the half with Chevalier and St Stephen has complete autonomy as a work of art.

Even in death man could assert a claim to living importance. An intimate vitality invests the modest monument of a fifteenth-century canon in Strasbourg Cathedral [21], a sculptural statement of Fouquet's theme which is even more

21. Conrad von Busnang Monument. Nicolaus Gerhaerts von Leyden

direct, by Nicolaus Gerhaerts von Leyden. Here the figure commemorated is so closely bound up in mood and composition with the Virgin and Child that the whole monument exudes a family cheerfulness and earthy robustness. There is no visionary air to the Virgin or the Child who playfully leans forward to touch the canon's fingers with his own; and there is nothing defunct about the canon still bursting with good health, who might serve as a prototype for Dickens's Canon Crisparkle – so well does that name convey the glistening *bonhomie* of Gerhaerts's portrait.

It was not everywhere that the dead lived so vividly, and *virtù* was sometimes to be emphasized more than *vivacità*. Decorum and truth to physical fact might prefer to retain the medieval deathbed image, rather than anticipate the Baroque monument where so often the dead live with a marble vitality greater than any they can have possessed in life. And between the two comes the procession of kneeling or standing figures, especially on French royal tombs, at prayer for eternity, set in dignified pious state over the shrivelled, naked fact of their bodily mortality. Already in the Early Renaissance there are stirrings on the cold slab of tomb; the image is sometimes alive enough, even if somewhat melancholy, to sit up and read a book – as does Don Martin Vazquez de Arce on his tomb at Sigüenza [22], watched by a page crouched at his armoured feet. In such a depiction, there is a neat mean

22. Tomb of Martin Vazquez de Arce (and detail).
Attributed to Sebastian de Almonacid

between the utter repose of death and a completely living, active image: a typically balanced Renaissance statement which achieves its effect by avoiding extremes. It remains portraiture rather than funerary monument. It does not set the subject within so fully dignified a framework as that preferred particularly at Florence for the tombs of distinguished men.

There the deathbed was interpreted suavely, a sleep softened by the overhead presence of the Virgin and Child in a heavenly vision (never in such proximity as Gerhaerts's friendly group had been), and made illustrious too by the sense of mourning earth below. The bier and sleeper are placed between these two levels – which indeed remain the theoretic fixed points of all funerary concepts. At the top of the huge tomb which Julius II was to plan for himself, and Michelangelo to design, it was originally intended that there should be two angels: one laughing 'as though rejoicing that the soul of the Pope should be received among the blessed spirits', while the other angel wept 'as though mourning that the world should be deprived of such a man'. That idea of double immortality is already present in Bernardo Rossellino's monument of the mid fifteenth century for the distinguished humanist Chancellor of Florence, Leonardo Bruni [23]. Although attached to the wall, it is conceived as a complete chapel, fully and firmly architectural (with none of that drama of looped-up tent-like curtains which had appeared in the prototype of this type of tomb, that by Donatello and Michelozzo, for the deposed Pope John XXIII, executed some twenty years earlier).

Bruni's body lies in a rich funerary chapel, rich in decoration and in allusion too. The city, antiquity, and religion are all assembled to mourn and to commemorate the man – himself depicted in simple dress, but with a strongly characterized physiognomy sufficiently turned towards the spectator to be easily seen. The simplicity of the depiction is itself proud; Bruni needs no greater adornment than a laurel crown, and he clasps nothing but a book. Intellectual distinction, not rank, is emphasized. So much for the physical appearance of the man. Above him is the perspective of Christian immortality: a roundel of Virgin and blessing Child, which symbolizes his heavenly reception. Below the bier is his sarcophagus, on which winged Genii, not angels but graceful yet daemonic, inspired forms, hold up an incised epitaph which eloquently

23. Leonardo Bruni Monument. Bernardo Rossellino

speaks the language of antiquity, evoking a deliberately non-Christian mythology, putting a modern Florentine back into the world of Homer, Plato, Virgil – one single world of the classical past, where at Bruni's death 'the Greek and Latin Muses could not restrain their tears'. Thus a whole sacred and profane framework is built round a man's existence, not dramatically but in terms of monumental architecture combined with sculpture, suggesting permanence and immortality by its consciously static harmony. Art has given fame, as well as preserving it. In the same way it has given it, more generously because less deservedly, to the young Cardinal of Portugal who happened to die at Florence, and on whom the Virgin and Child now smile down [24] – positively

24. *Virgin and Child.* Antonio Rossellino, with assistants

flown into his chapel (itself a complete building), borne up in a wreath of fruit and flowers, cherubs' heads, and stars, by dashing angels. This elaborately wrought polychromed shrine, designed by Bernardo's brother Antonio Rossellino, really reverses the idea of commemorating renown by a monument; the chief thing for which the Cardinal of Portugal is renowned is his chapel, and there is a certain aptness in the fact that the effigy of him is the least remarkable, least original, concept amid so much busy, proto-Baroque imagery.

It was at Venice, where probably an ineradicable artistic Aristotelianism always preferred facts to ideals, and physical truth to Neo-Platonic mysticism, that men lived after death most impressively; sometimes mounted on tombs which have ceased to be marble expressions of grief and become triumphal arches, dominated by the hero himself. Here it was rulers, above all, who were commemorated. Even where the Doge is shown as a passive deathbed image, his monument is usually alive with warrior-guards and he himself appears again, kneeling before the Virgin and Child. Some active image is nearly always present. Soldiers of three generations support the funeral *arca* on which Doge Pietro Mocenigo stands like some warrior-saint [25], embodying personal command and public victory. In this climate of Venetian State pride there is room for the individual but not much for Christian imagery – still less for humanistic learning. Antiquity is located, if anywhere, in Imperial Rome: a hard, masculine world of valour, discipline, leadership, which had been given stony shape in Mantegna's art, where it already seems to have become sculpture. That was a dream of Rome, just as Doge Mocenigo enshrines a dream of Venice: always triumphant and always prepared, magnificent, resolute, and commanding. There he stands, the largest figure on the monument – not peacefully swooning, hands clasped in death – but with shrewd and individualized features, his head tilted to face the next challenge, armoured and in ducal robes. No winged Genii but warlike youthful pages accompany him, their mood as keen and vital as his own; and six defensive warriors in niches guard this central group.

Like the Venetian Republic which he represents, Doge Mocenigo seems immortal; what is commemorated is *virtù* attaching to the State as well as to the man. Both are victorious; and it is not in any marked spirit of Christian charity that his sarcophagus is tersely inscribed with an explanation of who

25. Doge Pietro Mocenigo Monument. Pietro Lombardo, with assistants

26. Head of a Warrior: Doge Andrea Vendramin Monument.
Tullio Lombardo

paid for the whole splendid triumph which, thanks to the
Lombardi family of sculptors, animates a wall in the Church
of SS Giovanni e Paolo: 'from enemy spoils'. It is true that
the monument is topped by the blessing figure of Christ as
Redeemer, but that no more diminishes the mood of secular
certainty than does the church itself, the setting for so many
monuments of Venetian belief in the splendours – rather than
the miseries – of earthly life. There is proud bellicosity, not
piety, in the stern guard devised by Tullio Lombardo for the
Vendramin Monument [26]. Little shift of emphasis is felt
in the sixteenth-century monument of Doge Leonardo
Loredan, which in turn looks forward to the fully Baroque

splendours of the combined monument to the Doges Bertucci and Valier where four *putti* are sufficient to support one of the largest marble curtains in the world, the richest of all backdrops for Venetian rulers. That exaggerated gesture comes, of course, from a period of theatrically grand manner, against which the Lombardi-designed tombs are stoic; they are not concerned to flatter, and the martial allusions of the Mocenigo Monument are tribute to the sheer facts of Doge Pietro's victorious career. His tomb is history, not rhetoric – literal history which in bas-reliefs on the *arca* shows his entry into Scutari and his giving the keys of Famagusta to Caterina Cornaro.

27. Tombstone of Ludovico Diedo

For the services to the State of an individual who was not a Doge tribute could be paid in the same High Roman-Renaissance fashion, though on a lesser scale. A beautiful tombstone [27] of *niello*-work (also in SS Giovanni e Paolo) thus commemorates Ludovico Diedo who saved the Venetian Fleet at Constantinople in 1453. This might indeed have almost been designed by Mantegna, with its twin children who partly support Diedo's coat of arms and raise above it two splendidly decorated helmets, all contained within a graceful, ornamental arch. The effect is rich and yet unconfused, a design which – rather like the best *tarocchi* or playing-cards – relies on linear brilliance and barely suggests a third dimension. There is no portrait of Diedo, but there is instead celebration of his *virtù*, a heraldic triumph in which victorious achievement can be sensed in the curling fronds of mantling that wave like banners, and in the tall crests, one serpentine and winged, the other a satisfyingly plotted orrery, a perfect sphere. Like their supporters, the crested helmets balance within the curved space of archway, and the whole design achieves the status of a work of art. It is instinct with immortality – the immortality of a man's brave deeds – and the pride of bearing arms.

Elsewhere other monuments offer the double effigy, where a man can live again in vivid, 'engaged' portraiture. Although Pope Innocent VIII lies in one image recumbent on his tomb sculpted by Antonio del Pollaiuolo, he lives in the benevolently impressive, arresting, seated image which originally was placed below it [28] – thus close to the spectator, to whom it so eloquently speaks. He is not dead at all but

28. Pope Innocent VIII Monument (detail). Antonio del Pollaiuolo

actively blessing, turned on his chair with the very twist of natural gesture and clasping in his other hand a relic that was also a personal present, the blade of St Longinus's Holy Lance which had been sent to him by the Sultan of Turkey. The forceful image already trembles on the brink of the Baroque; the upraised hand and turned head, and even the thick fold of bronze robe thrown over the knee, are in themselves natural, undramatized forms but ones which will provide the language to be spoken imperiously by Bernini's *Urban VIII*. In comparison with that, Pollaiuolo's Innocent VIII remains homely; he is more Vicar of Christ than prince of the Church. The allegorical figures about him reflect aspects of a character concerned with ethics rather than with intellect or the arts. Unlike his predecessor Sixtus IV, whose tomb was also executed by Pollaiuolo, he could not be depicted in a monument where the Virtues are accompanied by the Liberal Arts. Charity is the dominant virtue of his tomb, and though it could perhaps hardly be claimed as the cardinal virtue of Innocent's life or pontificate, he was notable for his benevolence and ease of manner. Both are vividly suggested in Pollaiuolo's intensely human depiction: probably the most natural and accessible, as well as vital, image that had so far been sculpted of any Pope.

But the Renaissance was increasingly concerned to find fresh forms to express more than just living man seen reflected in the privacy of personal, private works of art. The 'living' image of Innocent VIII did not inspire comparable papal tombs in his successors. Vespasiano da Bisticci had written his biographies in the 'natural' style of his own native language and they remained private – never being published until the nineteenth century. He thought of them as rough material from which a more dignified form could be modelled. One of the reasons why he wrote was with a view to anyone wishing later to produce official and monumental lives in Latin. If it had not been for men like Livy and Sallust, he said, the renown of Scipio Africanus would have perished. The example of the ancients was not in itself to be enough for the Renaissance; the forms that they had, or might be supposed to have used, must also be revived. Historical collections of 'lives' and biographies of famous men combined with revival of the epic poem, producing rivals to the *Æneid* in a *Sforziad* or a *Borgiad*, even a *Christiad*, as well as cultivation of a distinguished Latin epistolary and essay style.

29. *Sir John Hawkwood*. Uccello

30. Design for a Monument to Gian Galeazzo Sforza. Filarete

In art one of the most elaborate of comparable forms, the equestrian statue, is probably the most famous example – though in fact Early Renaissance statues of that kind are rare and must always have been very expensive projects; a simulated statue in paint might serve instead [29]. It is perhaps significant that nothing came of Pollaiuolo's bold preference, when asked to execute a bronze bust of a patron, that he would rather make an equestrian statue of him – riding '*un chaval grosso*'. Ideas of equestrian triumph easily lent themselves to decoration [31], and many more seriously planned commemorations remained just projects, like Filarete's almost Assyrian-massive monument to Gian Galeazzo Sforza [30]. That would not, however, have shown Sforza in classical costume, unlike Donatello's equestrian monument of Gattamelata at Padua which is in many ways untypical [83]. The appearance there of a modern *condottiere* in antique costume was specifically condemned by Filarete, not for any reason connected with

31. Majolica Dish.
Jacopo Fattorini

religion (as could have been possible, given the statue's relationship to the Santo where Gattamelata is buried) but on the typical grounds of unverisimilitude. You should represent a modern man, Filarete advised, in the clothes he usually wears. Such advice is the more interesting because Filarete (with his adopted Greek name 'lover of virtue') might otherwise easily be supposed to have antique-humanist aspirations which would emphasize classical dignity rather than topical truth.

Exceptional circumstances, and exceptional artists, could produce dramatically new ways to enshrine a man's achievement, drawing on antique examples but producing quite fresh effects. The most ambitious of these naturally revolved round princely patrons since they alone could afford the expense. Nothing can compare with the ambitions and the part-achievement of Sigismondo Malatesta's temple at Rimini [32] where his name survives thanks to the combined

32. The Tempio Malatestiano
(S. Francesco, Rimini). Alberti

talents of Alberti, Agostino di Duccio, and Piero della Francesca. But that building was already thought of at the time as quite exceptional. Although instigated by less wildly pagan beliefs than was once supposed, it seemed blasphemous enough to Sigismondo's enemy Pope Pius II, himself occupied in building a self-monument of a more extensive kind in the town of Pienza [33]. Filarete had written of a rather fairy-tale kind of city, Sforzinda, which might be built by his patron Francesco Sforza. Pius II changed the name of his birthplace (Corsignano) to Pienza in his own honour, and when he rebuilt the Cathedral there stipulated that it should remain as

33. Piazza Pio II, Pienza. Bernardo Rossellino

he left it, with no alterations, additional monuments, or new chapels; even the colour of the walls must never be changed.

But Pius's basic creation was ideally classical, a cool piece of town-planning quite free from the reckless, deeply romantic and personal associations which stamp the Tempio Mala-stestiano with unique individuality. Pienza happens to be a monument to a Pope's concern with his name; the buildings erected there by Bernardo Rossellino urge one to inquire not about the patron but about the talented architect. At Rimini the basic concept is so bizarre – everything prompting a doubt as to what it means – that the patron's nature and his wishes seem the only key to it all. The whole project is indeed a subject in itself, one which remains complex and baffling. Yet it was patently biographical – concerned to celebrate the victories of Sigismondo Malatesta in love more than in war, to eternize his fame, and to serve as a pantheon. Just as at Urbino Federigo da Montefeltro was shown in the centre of his court of humanists and scholars,. and at the Vatican Sixtus IV was shown with his librarian and biographer Platina [34], so at Rimini the philosophers and humanists

34. *Platina before Pope Sixtus IV.* Melozzo da Forli

of the Malatesta Court were to be buried in sarcophagi under the arcades constructed along the outside walls. Over the whole building was intended to rise a conscious reminiscence of the outstanding pagan temple, the Pantheon at Rome, in a great dome which – arched above like the eternity of heaven – would shelter Malatesta and his beloved Isotta and their court. Far from challenging Christianity, the concept behind the Tempio seems to seek to synthesize Christianity with antiquity; both the Saints and the Planets find their places in the scheme; the 'temple' is also a Roman Catholic church. Yet the wish to synthesize may indicate awareness of the need for a new perspective, for the accepted doctrine to receive support from some fresh source. Poet, soldier, lover, as well as ruler, Sigismondo Malatesta was not a theologian, nor a philosopher; he employed such people and was prepared to allot them sarcophagi, along with those for a bishop and some doctors. He believed in all faiths, worshipping his ancestors (supposed to go back to Scipio) as much as his patron saint, and trusting in astrology as well as in religion – and, perhaps most of all, in the power of art [35].

The Tempio Malatestiano is a magic building, an idea almost more medieval than Renaissance, a palace of art that might have been described in some chivalric romance, with its emphasis on Sigismondo and Isotta: that ever-running, ever present motif, now lightly incised and now carved out to make a marble balustrade, of the S lovingly entwined about the I, until it seems hardly fanciful to read it as a triumphant Italian affirmative. Although Isotta was not yet dead, Sigismondo has, as a great medieval French poet had written, prepared her obsequies in the minster of love ('*dedans le moustier amoreux*') which he created out of what had been merely the church of S. Francesco at Rimini.

Like King Alfonso's Triumphal Arch at Naples, the Tempio Malastestiano represents a highly personal and highly ambitious creation, where an imaginative interpretation of antiquity provided the basic concept, leaving the execution quite 'modern' and unmistakably Renaissance. Such monuments are physically in contrast, but in other ways similar, to the miniature enshrining of *virtù* and *vivacità* in the portrait medal. As an art form this was virtually a Renaissance creation, inspired most patently by antique coins but purely commemorative in intention. How closely the portrait medal belonged in the ethos of Alfonso of Aragon and Sigismondo

Malatesta is shown by the fact that both these rulers fostered it, and both were incisively portrayed by its greatest practitioner, Pisanello. In this form very few inches of metal held the promise of eternity. Not only physical appearance but something of the personality too might be suggested by the medal's reverse where an allegorical allusion or an emblem could portray mental characteristics. And on Pisanello's marvellous medals – where the reverse often is even more brilliantly vivid than the obverse – there is always prominently imprinted his own proud statement of creation: '*Opus Pisani Pictoris*'. At once a new artifact but with antique echoes, personal, naturalistic and yet allusive, easily portable yet particularly durable, the portrait medal is a perfect symbol of Renaissance endeavour and achievement.

Part of its suitability as a symbol comes from the range of people portrayed. It rapidly widened from being of only rulers and princes to include that prominent category of scholars and humanists which took up so large a portion of Vespasiano da Bisticci's *Lives*. With them renown was not based on rank; they had not inherited devices or coats of arms, and thus a personal emblem could more freely be designed to accompany their portrait. Even when they did happen to possess arms, they preferred to have shown something more intimately related to their interests or their philosophy. The medal of Alberti has a winged eye on its reverse; that of Pico della Mirandola the Three Graces; that of Mantegna's Marchese Gonzaga a seated Cupid and the surprising words '*Noli Me Tangiere*' [sic]. Nearly every portrait medal had a reverse with some sort of allusive device, and it was an effective departure from this custom when the

36. Guarino da Verona. Matteo de' Pasti

74

medal of Marsilio Ficino, the great Florentine Platonic philosopher, bore on its reverse no device but only the single word 'Plato'.

Teachers could now be immortalized in a form – half-way between classical coin and gem – which had once served for emperors. Indeed, it is like a Roman emperor that one of the earliest and most distinguished of humanist teachers, Guarino da Verona, appears on his medal by Matteo de' Pasti [36]; it seems right that among the codices he owned should be an *Imperatorum vitae*. On the new coinage of scholarship, he is proudly stamped as a ruler: bare-headed and bull-necked, with his ugly but impressive profile filling most of the medal's area. The thick neck is accentuated by brief indications of – not contemporary costume but classical dress, a hint of the toga that accords well with the stylized short hair, at first glance seeming to contain amid it a laurel wreath. Not magnificence but plain dignity, and plain fifteenth-century costume, marks Pisanello's medal image of another outstanding teacher, Vittorino da Feltre [37], who had a school at Mantua. Here the Gonzaga were educated, but poor boys were also trained. The establishment was almost as much concerned with ethics and good behaviour as with pure scholarship. The standards were virtually those to be set up by Colet when founding St Paul's School early the following century: '. . . to increase knowledge, and worshipping of God and Our Lord Jesus Christ, and good Christian life and manners in the children'.

Vittorino's devotion to his pupils is allegorized on the reverse of the medal [38] in a crisply compact design of a pelican in its piety, feeding its young by pecking at its own

37. *Vittorino da Feltre.* Pisanello

38. *Pelican in its Piety* (reverse of medal 37)

breast. That was no far-fetched comparison, because there are many testimonies to his inspired tuition and affectionate care of the children entrusted to him. Though in effect a schoolmaster, but one of near-genius, he spoke with all the proud independence of a scholar respected in an age encouraging scholarship. Invited by the Marchese of Mantua to take the post of tutor to the Gonzaga children, he had laid down the condition that he would serve only so long as the Marchese's life commanded respect. That this high-mindedness was not a mere piece of rhetoric he showed in the discipline of his school, where the Marchese's children were treated like any others, and there was equality, as well as simplicity, in the style of living. The environment of his school is suggested by its pleasant name La Giocosa, and we know that it was suitably decorated with frescoes of children at play. The importance of education and upbringing is something realized in the Renaissance with quite fresh emphasis; yet what mattered most was the quality of the controlling individual. While the pelican in its piety sums up the attitude of mind with which Vittorino da Feltre approached his task, his intellectual distinction is expressed in the large letters of encircling inscription: '*Pater Mathematicus et omnis Humanitatis*'. Teacher but not writer, he had gained great reputation as a mathematician at Padua, where also his study particularly of Latin had made him outstanding. What Pisanello's medal commemorates is the modern man of renown, distinguished by intellect not rank, outwardly simple (Vittorino's dress is said to have contrasted with the customary splendour of clothes in the Veneto) but inwardly rich, taking his place in the long gallery of the great extending back to Pericles.

And though the light relief of the portrait medal is perhaps hardly sculpture as Pliny had meant it, his claim for sculpture's power to make men of renown yet more renowned comes to be pointedly justified by it. Indeed, it is perhaps finally more economically effective than the portrait bust itself, which – though so patently inspired by Roman examples – was slower to develop. The first dated portrait bust seems to be Mino da Fiesole's of Piero de' Medici [39], executed only two years or so before Pisanello's death. The people portrayed by medallists as gifted as Pisanello, or his follower de' Pasti, have been given an immortality in art, an enduring fame, which challenges merely historical importance. That Early Renaissance preoccupation with what people looked like had found

39. *Piero de' Medici*. Mino da Fiesole

a typically Renaissance form in which to express this concern.
And by its choice of people to record in that way it introduced
a new standard of ordinary human interest into art. When the
High Renaissance came, the medal, soon to decline altogether,
became too official and courtly to concern itself any longer
with such persons as Nonnina Strozzi, a late-fifteenth-century
Florentine woman whose likeness is conveyed with memorable linear effectiveness – though she is recorded merely as
the wife of the utterly obscure Bernardo Barbigia. About the
same time an unknown medallist immortalized the quite
unknown Alessandro de Paganotti, a middle-aged Florentine
man, whose bony wrinkled features seem to have the palpitating quality of life – so vividly characterized that one easily
forgets one knows only his profile and has never seen the
full face. Such people claim our interest not on account of
any particular *virtù* but by the more potent spell of *vivacità*.

3

For Art's Sake

It is sometimes tempting to see a shift from medieval to Renaissance conditions in the idea of the artist working no longer in the service of God but in that of an imperious individual or a patron with pronouncedly individual plans. It is certainly true that with the growth of autocratic Courts, and rising nationalism, artists of all kinds found themselves bent to execute highly personal projects with which they might well be out of sympathy. Yet, obliquely, this represented the prestige which art had obtained and which made patrons like Isabella d'Este or the Emperor Maximilian anxious to enlist art's services in fulfilling private fantasies and whims of their own. It is not surprising that with the growth of demands on the artists, occasionally tightening into positive demands for propaganda, there should come also a tendency for the artist to withdraw from the whole system and cultivate *his* individuality, and even his eccentricity. North and south of the Alps the tendency is first represented most patently by Dürer and Leonardo, self-aware, self-absorbed, ultimately their own patrons, with the freedom to execute nothing if they so wished. It was itself a new awareness that made Leonardo write down the significant precept: 'If you are alone you belong entirely to yourself' ('*tu sarai tutto tuo*'). When at the end of the fifteenth century the great Flemish composer Josquin des Prez was in the service of the Duke of Ferrara, the Duke's secretary proposed his being replaced by a less distinguished colleague. 'It is true that Josquin composes better,' he wrote, 'but he does it when it suits him and not when one wishes him to.' Possibly Josquin's peripatetic career indicates that other patrons remarked his independence; the composer's last years were spent as a Canon of Sainte-Gudule at Brussels and Provost of the Chapel at Condé – and there he may have felt secure, committed to obeying only his own inspiration. There is the additional aptness of independence in the comparison later made between him and Michelangelo as two artists who had achieved a unique position.

The comparison occurs in Cosimo Bartoli's *Ragionamenti accademici* (published at Venice in 1567); among their achievements is that of opening 'the eyes of all who delight in these arts . . .'.

Delight in the arts was, perhaps, to be of more significance in the Renaissance than the apparent autonomy of the artist; this was not to develop but rather to decline, sharply curtailed in, for instance, Baroque Rome and Louis XIV's Paris. But it was the autonomy of the work of art that really mattered. Even when employed by a specific patron, the Renaissance artist did not always have to serve the old duality of Church and State. Gradually, a work of art could find its justification simply in being itself. By the early sixteenth century *invenzione* was consciously challenging nature, and art was to be that which went beyond imitation:

> O'er picturing that Venus where we see
> The fancy outwork nature.

It could almost be symbolized by one of Andrea del Sarto's most ephemeral, indeed positively edible, works of art: an octagonal church which had a pavement of jelly, columns of sausages, a choir-desk of veal with a pastry book, and choristers of roasted thrushes, pigeons, and larks. This was executed not for some princely banquet given by a Burgundian nobleman but merely as one of several ingenious dishes devised by a group of Florentine artists to amuse themselves at a private dining club.

That may be an extreme demonstration of art in the service of giving pleasure, but it is worth noting that Sarto's church sounds as if it were quite a 'modern', centrally-planned building. Although the sophisticated surprise element in this creation is more typical of later developments, the idea of the work of art that serves no ulterior purpose is essentially a Renaissance one. It was to condition the creation and re-creation of several art forms, ranging from new categories of picture to the bronze statuette, as well as fostering certain musical developments. Thus, the *fantasia* or fancy (often called a *ricercar*) was an instrumental piece which retained thematic unity; but it was as much an encouragement of the composer's inventive imagination as, *mutatis mutandis*, Leonardo's advice to the painter to look into the stains on walls and see there an infinite number of things. Leonardo himself provided an aural parallel, mentioning the way in which one hears names in the sound of church bells. The sixteenth-century English composer Morley defined the fancy as 'When a musician taketh a point at his pleasure, and wresteth and turneth it as he list, making either much or little of it as shall seem best in his conceit'. And he goes on: 'In this more art may be shown than in any other music, because the composer is tied to nothing [Morley mentioned that he is 'without a ditty'] but he may add, diminish or alter at his pleasure.' Certain kinds of visual art were to possess exactly this freedom, dispensing with specific literary or religious subject-matter and purpose, serving instead as adjuncts to pleasant surroundings.

It is no accident that the popular medium of the engraving – where for the first time duplication of a work of art was the very essence of it, removing the concept of a single 'original' – was also the medium which encouraged free fantasy. Like a musician, the artist could take 'a point at his pleasure', as Antonio del Pollaiuolo and Mantegna did, and supremely Dürer, and by his invention around it demonstrate the brilliant fecundity of his art. We are confronted by engravings where the subject-matter is perfectly clear, where a thematic unity is preserved, but where there is no reference beyond what we see. Action is preferred: Pollaiuolo engraved a battle of naked men; the sculptor Bertoldo executed a battle relief which equally is not illustrative of a specific incident. Nothing is illustrated except the artist's vision which often contains a quite deliberate element of the fantastic. The point of Dürer's engraving *Sea-Monster Abducting a Woman* [40] is that it is in disaccord with our own normal experience. In so far as it tells a story, it is a tall one – literally expressed in the sweeping height of castle-crowned rock – but it tells this with every possible device of art so that it seems, is, real in the dimension of art. Nearly every feature in it can be claimed to derive from Dürer's natural observation; the buildings hint at Nuremberg and it is noticeable that the woman's head-dress is late fifteenth-century German. The most remarkable effect is in the study of the female nude – appearing here for virtually the first time in non-religious German art. In some ways, it is this anatomy that is Dürer's 'subject': a scrupulously delineated if not very pleasing body, the smooth pale flesh of which is contrasted with the dark, rugged skin of the juxtaposed monster. She is one of those Venus-figures whose calm nudity is itself a Renaissance achievement. The centre of the composition, and the dominating motif of it, is something justified simply by interesting the artist; having established this truth, he surrounds it by minor factual details which also interest him and which he wishes to assemble into an arbitrary and fantastic total composition. There might almost be a concealed allegory of art in the 'truth to nature' of the woman who is borne up and along by the power of the imagined creature; each needs the other in the perfect marriage of observation and invention that – for the Renaissance – was art.

Amid the sophisticated fantasy there is perhaps even some spark of humour, or at least a deliberately non-psychological portrayal, because the woman seems strangely relaxed and barely disturbed at being borne away on the sea-man-monster's finny tail. The basic incident probably belongs deep in folk-lore, but Dürer has made of it something quite 'modern', technically a *tour de force* of engraving, with throughout the varying effect of textures and surfaces conveyed, and alternation of areas heavily worked in detail with those left utterly blank. Part of the serene sense of the needle-pointed castle towers on the high hill comes from their being set against a great white expanse of unadorned cumulus cloud. That restraint contrasts with passages of worked elaboration – like that of the varied-foliaged trees that fringe the shore, or the minute distant galleon with its chequered sails.

The refinement, and even the touch of travesty, in Dürer's attitude to a piece of antique folk-lore can be paralleled by the Renaissance literary attitude to the old-style chivalric tale, once despised but brought back with courtly glosses by Luigi Pulci, then by Boiardo and finally – at its most polished, most courtly, and artificial – by Ariosto. In their poems there is the same varied, brilliant, intricate texture woven around quite trivial romantic adventures of knights and ladies, encounters with monsters, visits to enchanted castles. Yet the real similarity lies in the freedom taken by the poets, as by the artist, to treat the 'subject' just as they like. Ariosto was a close contemporary of Dürer's. The two men were very different in situation and character, and yet the *Orlando Furioso* is, in point of atmosphere, the best literary parallel to Dürer's engraving. In both we are plunged into a complete cosmos in which delight in invention and the sheer skill of the creator matter more than any verisimilitude; detail on detail accumulates, always with the intention of increasing

40. *Sea-Monster Abducting a Woman*. Albrecht Dürer

41. *Nude Youth Holding a Rearing Horse.* Studio of Filippo Lippi

our wonder. As much as Astolfo on the hippogryph in Ariosto's poem, we are sent travelling by Dürer. Ours is a bird's-eye view of some coast that might be washed by the Indian Ocean, where the castle could belong to the enchantress Alcina, and where it would be in key with the whole exotic mood for something to rear up suddenly in the waves and prove to be a whale:

> . . . la maggiore
> Che mai per tutto il mar veduta fosse.

The same magic liberty allows the whale in the poem to bear off Astolfo and Alcina for further adventures and makes it seem quite natural that Dürer's sea monster should accommodate the reclining woman who may herself well be some marine enchantress rather than a victim. One might even feel that she is returning to her own element – a visual hint towards that idea given perhaps in her drapery that flows smoothly down until transmuted into ripples of the waves. Passively yet half-sadly, she gazes back at the agitated human beings – already become distant small figures – while being borne firmly away towards the open sea and new experiences.

Engraving was a modern medium, an invention of the fifteenth century, but other more traditional art forms now enabled artists to dodge out of the restrictions of large-scale formal commissions with a freedom that had always been possible for poets and musicians. It was, significantly, as a revival of an antique prototype that the bronze statuette evolved, dealing with pagan subject-matter for purely decorative purposes at a time when independent paintings of such themes still remained comparatively rare. Antique coins, gems, and such small classical bronzes as were known provided prototypes. Literary references were probably equally if not more powerful in evoking highly finished small bronzes, encouraging the creation of works that eventually shifted from imitation into the full freedom of timeless subjects. This freedom is already felt in some drawings based on antique sculpture [41]. It is quite obvious in the small statuettes of horses that derive from Leonardo's designs. These are associated by Vasari with the sculptor Rustici, a friend of Leonardo's who possessed the proper temperament, and inherited sufficient money, to afford artistic independence. After a quarrel with some magistrates over the value of one of his works he resolved to design in future 'only for individuals'. His statuettes of horses were chiefly in 42. *Apollo*. Antic private houses, and though artistically indebted to Leonardo, they were also inspired probably by Rustici's own love of animals, a trait of his character that Vasari thought worth emphasizing.

With the bronze statuette there can exist a degree of duplication that links it somewhat to the medium of engraving; casts could be taken from clay or wax models, as probably happened with the Leonardo-derived statuettes of horses. Here it was the artist's own personal interests which could find expression in the statuette. But the development of collectors' and patrons' interest in owning such small-scale objects was also significant. Statuettes were essentially to be lived with, to be handled or in some way utilized in daily life. They were deliberately scaled down, so that an antique life-size statue could become in a miniature copy the ornament for table or shelf [42]. While they could, and often did, take religious subjects for treatment, most of the memorable small bronzes [43] inhabit a climate akin to Dürer's engraving *Sea-Monster Abducting a Woman*. Like that, they are really concerned with anatomical study, seeking opportunities to create not only the graceful body in repose but often preferring grotesque bodies in action.

Elements both of violence and fantasy that would have raised technical problems in marble or life-size bronze – and no doubt other problems where civic patronage was concerned – could be easily incorporated in the bronze statuette which developed from the pungent, naked force expressed by the *Hercules and Antaeus* [44] of Antonio del Pollaiuolo into the rich, nearly always deeply rustic, pagan world of Riccio, working chiefly in the following century. More virile than Virgilian, Riccio lets his fantasy play among Satyrs and Sphinxes; Pan is his presiding god and there is a frankly sexual sense in the freedom of nakedness, the surface of skin exposed to the open air – so that patina and sunburn seem in retrospect to have become nearly the same thing. Riccio's inkwells, door-knockers, and lamps [45] are objects that could be on no other scale; not models or reductions of large-scale work, not accidental statuettes, they are conceived in small yet splendid proportions, vigorously wrought but encouraging close examination. They share the same delight in inventiveness which characterizes Dürer and Ariosto, ingeniously refining on the commonplace 'subject' (object,

43. Inkwell. Severo da Ravenna

44. *Hercules and Antaeus.* Antonio del Pollaiuolo

rather) of receptacle for ink or oil by enriching this to the point where its function is not always immediately obvious. We must follow the artist and then enjoy the unexpected discovery that the mouth of a grotesque head is the inkwell's opening or that what seems a miniature boat becomes in fact a lamp. In place of the ordinary concept of a candlestick, Riccio will have a seated Satyr clasping a vase which serves to hold the candle; thus might a Renaissance scholar feel illuminated by antiquity.

After the masculine clash of Pollaiuolo's group, where antiquity is synonymous with violence and unleashed aggression, and the sculptor is concerned – in a statuette that could easily serve as model for life-size sculpture – with the truths of painful experience, Riccio may be seen speaking of a more marvellous past, providing him with motifs for endless fantasy and suggestive too of tender feelings. His group of

45. A Lamp.
Riccio

46. *Satyr and Satyress.* Riccio

Satyr and Satyress [46] is intimate and poignant, with a sympathetic response to these creatures that comes near the mood of Piero di Cosimo [47]. The subject is quite unlearned, easily comprehensible, and indeed quite commonplace. But it is also 'free', because no story is illustrated, no belief is involved – not even scholarly belief in the classical past – and no particular experience or knowledge is required of the spectator. The group does not even appear to have had any specific purpose; it is simply a work of art, as intimate in scale as in feeling, an imaginative exploration into a world alien from our own, represented by beings that are only partly human. Their wordless affectionate dialogue – very beautifully does Riccio suggest their dumb expressiveness – is what is emphasized, along with their complete absorption in each other. No longer does the Satyr represent base passion but a noble animality and an almost romantic trust in the promptings of love. It is the dream of a pagan world that never was, and the group is brushed by a wistful awareness that in reality this can never be.

Such a mood would be nearly impossible in a public commission, or in a large-scale piece of sculpture. It demands

47. *A Mythological Subject* (detail). Piero di Cosimo

privacy and argues patronage that welcomes a personal note in the resulting work of art. Those strains of the rustic and classical so apparent in Riccio and well summed up in the word 'pagan' (from *paganus* meaning 'of the country'), were to touch and combine in other fresh forms of art in Europe: encouraging the Giorgionesque style of picture, the 'new' poetry of Clément Marot in France (expressed in such autobiographical verses as those about his own childhood, *L'Enfance de Marot*), and several musical developments, led by Politian's brief drama with music, *Orfeo* (probably written for Mantua in 1480) which was the first vernacular play on a classical subject and also an important prototype in the literary use of pastoral motifs.

In these ways art of all kinds was seeking – and finding – new methods of involving people in its aura, postulating a climate of pleasure rather than instruction. A cupboard door [48] need not provide a geometrical pattern of inlay but could offer an early example of urban view. The decorative arts were no longer employed solely in the service of the Church or Princes but helped to make a prosperous citizen's environment agreeable and indeed 'artistic'. The small

48. View of Venice. Wood Inlay

bronze, the engraving, medals and coins, are only some of the more obvious adjuncts to such an environment, where the *objet d'art* and the curiosity – a Riccio statuette, antique pottery, and a branch of coral or piece of mineral – coexist on the same shelf [49], justified simply by giving pleasure to their owner. The decoration of plates and glasses was by the sixteenth century to become almost too elaborate, the plates losing that first heraldic boldness which stamps with linear

49. *St Augustine in his Study* (detail). Vittore Carpaccio

clarity beasts and profiles in simple colours on Florentine fifteenth-century majolica [50]. The merchant of Prato, Francesco Datini (who died in 1410) already owned a glass bowl 'very well worked in gold', probably made at one of the Italian glass factories, of which Venice became the most famous. The jewelled, enamelled richness of Venetian glass, still solid-looking in the fifteenth century [51], is a perfect symbol of the sensuous impact Venice was to require of all

50. Majolica Vase

51. Nuptial Goblet. Attributed to the Barovier family of glass-makers

52. Cassone with Solomon and the Queen of Sheba (?)

art; but this quality is planned and achieved by sophisticated means. Sensuousness must not be equated with brainlessness.

With such work there can no longer be any division into major and minor arts. Some of the painted furniture of the fifteenth century – wedding-chests [52] and birth-plates – was painted by great artists, several of them no less great for being anonymous to us. The Duke of Burgundy's goldsmith, Loyet, produced a wonderful reliquary at once realistic and exotic, part fantastic toy, part religious object – and fully a work of art [53]. An artist like Antonio del Pollaiuolo was active in ways other than as sculptor and painter, producing jewellery and vivid embroidery designs [54]. It is significant of the demand, as well as Pollaiuolo's ability to supply it, that Vasari speaks of his opening a magnificent goldsmith's shop where he executed waxes 'and other fancies in relief' ('*facendo di rilievo cere e altre fantasie*'): small objects freed from the constraints of commission, the artist's personal inventions which can become somebody's personal property.

One art in particular offered direct involvement, creating participants instead of mere spectators and collectors. This was music. Already free to some extent from the utilitarian, liturgical, or ceremonial bases of the visual arts, music in the Renaissance became the most popular form of art and it is, oddly enough, a tribute to its diffusion and to the widespread

53. Reliquary of Charles the Bold. Gérard Loyet

54. *The Execution of St John the Baptist.* After Antonio del Pollaiuolo

practice of it that no composer – not even Josquin des Prez – was to achieve during his lifetime the prestige of a Raphael or a Michelangelo. Nobody needed to argue the case for music. In Castiglione's famous book *Il Cortigiano* (published in 1528 but written some twenty years before) it is assumed that the courtier will be knowledgeable and proficient in music; however, it is necessary for Castiglione to explain that knowledge of painting is also useful, although it might seem ill-suited to a gentleman.

That sense of creating something new, breaking away from the medieval past, is as conscious in music as in the visual arts. Something as new as perspective was to be created too, in polyphony; and new uses of music in a social private context were possible with the invention of printed notation. It is significant that the very first publication of the first musical printing firm, Petrucci's at Venice (*Harmonice Musices Odhecaton* in 1501) consisted largely of French *chansons*, the form which was so strongly to influence the rising Italian counterpart, the madrigal. This is music for the home, a relaxed art shared by two or three people, not attached to any formal occasion but performed for sheer pleasure. Castiglione assumes a courtly well-bred atmosphere in which music has been absorbed and learnt almost unconsciously; for those who wanted to learn the practical rudiments, simply for private performance, manuals were now to be written which helped to dissolve mystery and made musical knowledge accessible to ordinary *bourgeois* people. Nothing comparable existed in other arts to Virdung's *Musica getutscht* ('Music rendered into German'), an instructional dialogue accompanied by woodcut illustrations. Music had the further advantage of being unhaunted by antique classical prototypes. Its prestige as a liberal art – being enshrined in the *Quadrivium*, along with Geometry, Arithmetic, and Astronomy – might derive from antiquity but it was not overshadowed by pressure to imitate the ancients. This provides yet one more example of the truth that Renaissance impetus did not derive directly from that source; in music, the demand was explicitly for what was *new* – in deliberate revolt against old musical styles. In 1477 the Flemish-born theorist Johannes Tinctoris, living at the Neapolitan royal court, emphasized this 'modern' reaction which is very similar in general terms to the feelings of humanists like Alberti about the visual arts: 'only during the last forty years have there been compositions which according to the experts are worth hearing . . . .' But where Alberti could look back to Giotto and then behind him to the legendary exploits of ancient painters like Zeuxis, Tinctoris found his oldest relevant composer in the Englishman John Dunstable who had died barely twenty-five years before.

And there is a further distinction, useful in reminding us again that the Renaissance was not by any means just an Italian phenomenon. Alberti thought of artistic developments almost entirely as Florentine; it is ultimately civic pride that leads him to celebrate Donatello, Masaccio, and Brunelleschi, while Florence remains for him 'this most splendid of cities'. For the musicians and musical theorists, on the other hand, their art had developed internationally – though the major impetus and the great composers had come from Northern Europe. Italy might employ and admire them – just as it did Flemish painters – but its own contribution was for long quite slight. Indeed, its first interesting creation was not strictly in the musical field at all but in the pictorial one of the concert painting, which evolved before the Italian madrigal though to some extent its visual equivalent.

The idea of art as pleasure-giving, which came only gradually to the visual arts, had long been present in music; it had in fact been the subject of actual attack by the Church, in the fourteenth century and earlier, exactly because of the tendency of melodies to intoxicate the ear. St Thomas Aquinas had disapproved of music in church; John of Salisbury said that it defiled the service of religion. An answer to these typical ecclesiastical sentiments is given by the French fourteenth-century composer and poet Machaut who defined music as 'a science, whose purpose is to make people laugh and sing and dance'. Even in music for very different purposes, like the accompanying of religious services, there were advances towards a more 'natural' and to some extent more realistic style. The use of secular melodies for Masses is no more irreligious than is the humanity stressed in Donatello's *St George*; in both cases, those who experienced these works did so with a sense of familiarity (the saint who is yet so like an ordinary man; the music at Mass which is yet based on a popular song, *Adieu Mes Amours*). Music was endeavouring freshly to express emotions, to mirror and communicate – sometimes by the naïve device of 'eye-music', where black notes might stand for grief, and sometimes by the sheet musical skill of the composer. There were pieces which positively imitated, ranging from birdsong to chattering women, and culminating in famous compositions like the *Battle* by the French composer Janequin who had actually been present at the battle of Marignano when in 1515 François I defeated the Swiss.

A more subtle realism and expressionism concerned the musical structure; exploitation of the lower ranges of sonority, giving a sense of greater depth, has been compared to the development of perspective in pictures and the growing concern in art with space. What is pleasing to ear and eye is the harmony that comes from all the parts being in proportion; and again Donatello's *St George* is relevant, with its innate sense of balance, its finishing of all details and yet avoidance of stress on any particular aspect. As a result, we experience a unified, total effect, in which all the parts are subordinated to the whole. In music the proportions changed from the Gothic thread of single voice to the weaving of voice with voice in what might seem haphazard as it began but gradually welded itself into a complex harmonic whole. A leading musical theorist of the early sixteenth century, Pietro Aron, speaks of the modern gain through composers having abandoned the successive manner of composition in favour of the simultaneous method. And development of method gave the composer new ways of expression, vivid enough to challenge the direct visual images that the artist could create.

There existed a double form of musical imitation; in the form of music itself, where use of counterpoint is deliberately imitative, and then in the reflection, through this texture, of emotional states of mind. It is not exterior sounds that are then copied, but a musical equivalent of an emotion is formed of it. The suffering face of Christ crucified was said to have been evoked in one of Josquin's motets more convincingly than could have been achieved by any painter; and since the writer of these words was a sixteenth-century Nuremberg printer, it is quite likely that he was thinking particularly of Dürer's images of Christ enduring the Passion. If that is so, the tribute to Josquin is all the greater and a further testimony to the highly emotional expressiveness contemporaries found in his music. Not surprisingly, Josquin was Luther's favourite composer, the choice, that is, of someone who was music-lover and composer himself, as well as reformer; and it was exactly the Flemish master's expressive power that Luther praised: 'Josquin is a master of the notes which must express what he desires. . . .'

It was the less serious and elevated musical forms, especially those that in one way or another combined words with music, which have the closest affinities with developing new strains in pictorial art: strains that are concerned with evading the tyranny of religious and portrait subject-matter. This freedom was already deeply embedded in music and literature, and it is not quite clear why painting took so long to produce forms comparable to the love-lyric, or the *frottola*, a sort of popular and lively little story that was sung. Not often in fifteenth-century painting is love represented by people in contemporary costume, and seldom with the easy-going exuberant manner of Cossa's fresco at Palazzo Schifanoia [55]. The *frottola* was

55. *The Month of April* (detail). Cossa

especially cultivated at Venice, the city which was to contribute most to the emancipation of painting and to create a painted version, in effect, of the love-lyric. When Titian's friend Aretino speaks fondly of music's power to unlock the doors of women's chastity, his words bring to mind paintings by Titian where a nude woman reclines while nearby an organ-player turns from his instrument towards her. Such pictures are High Renaissance celebrations, with punning wit as well as art, of sensual pleasure; the visual suggestiveness and erotic imagery would have appealed to Shakespeare, who at times does seem almost directly inspired by Titian's pictures.

Although music had early appeared in pictures, it was for long subordinated to religious themes, where the performers were angels who serenaded the central figures. It was a typically Renaissance revolution when the music-makers became ordinary men – and women – and their concert the complete subject of a picture. Ideas of harmony which were to be applied intellectually and mathematically in Renaissance architecture could also be expressed less learnedly in paintings where music (Shakespeare's 'food of love') easily became a metaphor of communication between man and woman. Such ideas were eventually to reach full subtlety in Watteau's art, but the concert pictures of the Renaissance already contain concepts of social harmony and intimate lovers' dialogues of music and song, with frequent depiction of that most popular of secular instruments, the lute.

Once again, it is by a shift of emphasis that the permanent human concern with music was made to yield a new and, in a special way, realistic expression. It was not music's dignified descent from Pythagoras and the ancients which now mattered so much as its social possibilities. Private concerts were painted where previously Orpheus and King David, or Music herself personified, had been the theme. Music went on accompanying processions and festivals, as it had always done and indeed continues to do. Its theory interested intellectual artists like Alberti and Leonardo; music could reveal the harmonic ratios which are inherent in nature and thus make accessible the secrets of that harmony which underlies, it was supposed, the universe. Not until Palladio perhaps was there a truly Pythagorean architect, but the principles of measure and harmonic proportion were recognized in the fifteenth century as common to music and

56. The Loggia del Consiglio, Verona

architecture. The results are such musically graceful buildings as the Loggia del Consiglio at Verona [56] – which really is like melody in stone. No wonder that a musical theorist, Gaforio, was called in at Mantua to advise about the Cathedral. '*Harmonia est discordia concors*' ('harmony is concordant discord') is the message which comes on a scroll from Gaforio's mouth in the frontispiece of his treatise on the harmony of instruments, where he is shown lecturing to a group of pupils, religious and lay.

Practice rather than theory animated the amateur musician – and most concert pictures reflect an amateur circle. Painters themselves were often musicians; Vasari mentions Giorgione's skill as lute-player and singer which recommended him to fashionable upper-class Venetians. He records of Sebastiano del Piombo that he was reputed to have been a singer and instrumentalist before he ever became a painter; Sebastiano was competent on all instruments but was specially fond of the lute. In England Sir Thomas Wyatt, accomplished lutanist and poet, was to make more than conventional references to music in his verse. Printed music and part-books, as well as manuals, were naturally to encourage the private, non-professional performer, less concerned with the laws of universal harmony than with an agreeable leisure-time activity which collected together a group of interested participants. This aspect of participating is itself important; it brought music directly into ordinary life, and the pictures that reflected this approximate to genre.

Among the strictest and least fanciful of a category that was quickly to become romantic and rather consciously idyllic is *A Concert* [57], painted by Lorenzo Costa – also one of the earliest of such pictures. Costa's people are typically fifteenth-century in their plain dress and serious demeanour; and the picture has an artistic concentration which matches that of the trio of singers. It is exact and truthful, as well as concentrated. There is the minimum of setting, and what there is suggests an interior, unlike the later preference for showing music-making in country surroundings. The composition is made up only of the performers and the objects they need for their performance – and that performance is the picture's subject. The three people are occupied in achieving concord: by keeping time, which they mark with their fingers, and by each voicing the correct but different note, indicated by the differing

57. *A Concert.* Lorenzo Costa

degrees of open mouth which the painter carefully records. In the sense of concord conveyed, Costa goes beyond facial recording. He has arranged the group so that it composes about the central performer whose lute visually dominates it, while the outer hands of the two subordinate performers imitate and visually balance each other – and thus a sort of pictorial counterpoint is conveyed. It is an additional interest, both visual and aural, that one of the trio should be a woman; and though the men sing without particular attention to her, her presence serves to relax the mood just a little. It is not yet the sort of picture where the lutanist sighs for his lady or woos her by his playing. Perhaps in some ways Costa's picture hints at a less extravagant and more sincere society where a woman may take her part as an equal, unambiguously respected, unlike an idol. What is suggested here is social friendliness in the tenderly intimate gesture of the woman's hand resting on the lutanist's shoulder – the sole indication any of the trio gives of the others' physical presence, and the more effective for being, quite literally, the only touch of this kind.

The picture becomes one more quintessence of many of its century's aims: in its human theme, its dignified truth-telling, its preference for factual statement rather than anything too rhetorical and ideal. It lacks the grace and richness, or the eloquence of the High Renaissance. It is not free from the didactic. Beside a Giorgione or a Titian, it would seem intensely prosaic and somewhat stiff. Costa's people might be made of glazed and polychromed wood, sharing the texture of the beautifully shaped lute, and no more animated than that, for all their expressive features. Yet it is a new art which has given them that very sense of solidity and reality, creating the illusion of space, first by the wide marble parapet (whose recession is conveyed by the steep perspective of the miniature fiddle) and then by the strongly modelled group behind it. Even in the quality of light which illuminates the picture there is dogged truthfulness; no shadows mitigate or blur the detail of the costumes, the strands of hair. Everything has a geometrical precision which is summed up at the picture's centre by the perfect, perforated rose of the lute, the fretted pattern of which is traced with Eyckian delight in its complex design. Throughout there is evidence of science: the painter's knowledge of, and ability to depict in an eye-deceiving way, external reality. There is also art: used here to serve no other ends than art itself – depicting people engaged in no ritual, religious or secular, and yet not content merely to reflect life, but rearranging it, recomposing it in the interests of art.

Costa's picture is more than genre, and it is tinged with its own sense of the ideal – a hint of timelessness being encouraged by the absolutely plain, undetailed setting which helps to emphasize the picture's concern with humanity. Perhaps it is no accident that the singers are anonymous; though quite strongly individualized, they remain performers, not just three people posing for a group portrait. Their importance comes from their activity – and so the picture is a new-style allegory of Music, personified now not by vaguely legendary heroes, gods, or Old Testament kings, but by modern, ordinary people. And music is seen pragmatically, not theoretically; it is a pastime and yet more than a pastime, a social activity which is also an art itself and an education. This sort of life, we may feel, is what the picture advocates. If it has a message, it is a tacit, ethical one, suggesting a society in which the revelation of art replaces religious revelation. By the aid of music man can achieve harmony and concord, with himself and with others. Such ideas may seem very fanciful until one recalls the stress which the Renaissance again and again laid on music, as pleasurable and as educative. Remembering how David soothed Saul, the Prior of Hugo van der Goes's monastery had plenty of music played to him in an attempt to banish his melancholia; it was thought worth recording that even then the painter's health did not improve.

Sir Thomas Elyot, the author of the humanist educational treatise *The Boke Named the Governour,* hardly exaggerates the importance attached to music when he speaks of the ideal tutor to the ideal young nobleman who 'shall commende the perfect understandinge of musike declarynge howe necessary it is for the better attaynynge the knowledge of a publike weale . . .'.

4

Humanism and Humanity

That bounding optimism once thought typical of Renaissance man in his attitude to himself (everyone his own Tamburlaine) was in fact not untypical of Renaissance man's attitude to the cosmos. The word's connotations in Greek of order – of perfect order – had led to its use first among ancient philosophers as the term for the world, a universe harmoniously planned and perfectly arranged – the world as a work of art – as opposed to unshaped, sprawling Chaos. This optimistic framework is what is constantly built round man especially in the Early Renaissance: the complete cohesion of natural and supernatural elements, mingled by God, which goes back to Plato's account of the creation of the world in the *Timaeus*. Renaissance optimism about man's place in this cosmos is not necessarily connected at all with ideas of his autonomy. Quite the opposite is the intention of the most famous discourse on the subject, Pico della Mirandola's *Oration on the Dignity of Man* – planned for delivery at Rome early in 1487 – which emphasizes man's power to rise out of his middle state and be reborn on a divine plane. It is thus man's uniquely marvellous potentiality which is stressed, and his beautifully sited place in the chain of being. He may disdain worldly things and aspire towards the Godhead; or he may sink into being dull and brutish. There is considerable optimism here, religious optimism of a kind similar to that which radiates from the paintings of Fra Angelico.

It is not quite true to say, though, as is still often said, that man is seen by Renaissance philosophers like Pico as at the centre of the universe, because for them the Godhead was still at its centre and life was still partly seen as a medieval pilgrimage, the world no abiding city but a temporary resting-place on the winding road up to the celestial city. When the young Thomas More translated into English the biography of Pico written by his nephew it was to provide a spiritual book; it is the account of an exemplary life, almost that of an uncanonized saint rather than anyone resembling a semi-pagan philosopher or daring intellectual. What More is concerned with is the teaching of one who 'cleaved to God in very fervent love' and who believed that reason served merely to confirm the Gospel.

Pico della Mirandola, about whom Voltaire was typically acute, became in the nineteenth century such a glamorous symbol of the Renaissance that it is worth pausing over him. Thanks to Burckhardt and Pater, he stood for all that was best in his period; and his learning, his good looks, and his premature death, helped to make him a figure of wistful elegance. When Burckhardt looked at him it was somehow to divine the lofty flight which Italian philosophy would have taken had it not been for the Counter-Reformation. For Pater, Pico was not only one who romantically tried to reconcile the pagan and Christian systems ('lying down to rest in the Dominican habit, yet amid thoughts of the older gods'), but someone whose outward form was an image 'of that inward harmony and completeness, of which he is so perfect an example'.

It may well be that Pico typifies his period, but he is more a mystic than a systematic philosopher – and to us he may seem more like Shelley than anyone else in his muddled ideas, too omnivorous learning, good looks, and early death. Pico's philosophy may emphasize man's capabilities but they are to be employed in his system to cast off the things of this world so that man can as quickly as possible pass on to a transcendent plane. Pico is typically Neo-Platonic in being un-visual. We might guess that he had less time than Savonarola – to whom religious content was all – for the artistic products of his period. If Florence was seething with new artistic events, he was indifferent to them. He was a scholar, concerned with books, not painting or sculpture; and though he may well have looked like a Botticelli angel, there is no reason to suppose he had any specific interest in the artist. He sought the truth of revealed religion in books beyond the Bible, invoking Plato, the Eleusinian mysteries, and the Cabbala, among others, in an attempt to synthesize all belief. His contemporaries seem to have been more impressed by the number of books he had read than by his ideas. Apollo and Bacchus for him are merely prefigurings of God, and his treatment of antiquity is largely in such nearly medieval terms, by which, for example, the cock ordered to be sacrificed by the dying Socrates sings daily 'in the twilight of morning with the morning stars as they praise God'. On this basis it is difficult to see what gave Burckhardt his comforting thoughts about Italian philosophical progress beyond Pico. The truth is that Pico, however attractive as a name, is a figure of transition, largely rooted still in the Middle Ages and far from advancing new ideas, really calling on the world to reform and repent. After Pico's death Savonarola told of Pico's vision of the Virgin who promised he should not die; and it is in such a climate of miraculous visions and anticipations of heavenly bliss – rather different, it should be noted, from the deathbed of Socrates – that Pico della Mirandola belongs.

The scholars and philosophers of the Early Renaissance are typified by limits of this kind, constrained indeed by them to the point where their teaching is either mystical or mildly ethical, and their serious contributions to philosophy as such non-existent. Great humanists of the period were men like the Spanish cardinal Ximenes, in some ways a prototype of More, who still held theology to be the queen of the sciences. It is a sort of intellectualism rather than real speculation which is common to these people, an intellectualism similar to that which in the arts fastened on problems of perspective. Florence was particularly a home of this type of cerebration, mentally equivalent to a passion for chess-problems, and scarcely of more relevance ultimately to human needs. Just as the world of Brunelleschi and Masaccio has little connexion with the developments of art in the world even of Titian, not to mention Rubens and Bernini, so the Florentine Platonists, and indeed Renaissance philosophers altogether, have virtually nothing to contribute to the speculations of a Descartes or Locke. However great their knowledge, and however many classical authors they might cite, they remained imprisoned within a theological concept, an electrified framework which could give a painful shock to those who pushed against its bars. Heresy was already detected in the pious writings of Pico della Mirandola, not surprisingly by a Church soon to punish the physical discoveries of Vesalius.

A peculiar flattery has given allure to the idea of Renaissance patronage of learning of all kinds. But what Pico in fact experienced was a bitter dangerous conflict with the Pope which lasted several years. The speculations on immortality of Pietro Pomponazzi, a few years later, were hardly better received by Renaissance officialdom, this time at Venice; by the order of the Patriarch and Doge, his book was burnt and he was there declared a heretic. Such examples are warnings against too generous an equation of the Renaissance with anything resembling happy pagan scepticism or encouragement of profound scrutiny of human nature. And it is not therefore surprising that the major artistic achievements of the period reflect an optimistic or at least outwardly conforming attitude. Whatever the private views of Leonardo da Vinci, his paintings manage – perhaps only just, one may feel – to preserve intact the Christian and Roman Catholic structure. Most other artists, sculptors, and architects do more than preserve it; it provides a structure which they are easily able to clothe and adorn, giving new plastic, pictorial, conviction to it. At least until the High Renaissance the Church provided not so much opportunities and instigation but invaluable subject-matter for every kind of artistic activity; it was a book in which artists were always glad to read.

Yet within apparently stiff covers, the emphasis of its text was changing in ways that were to affect artists. Even if knowledge might not press too recklessly into spheres of belief, still knowledge was valued as something desirable in itself. The new importance of libraries, the growth of them, the impetus to disseminated knowledge given by printing: these were all signs of the desire for information and a wish to know the truth of things. Man himself became a less passive creature, less the subject of revelation and more himself the one who revealed. Intellectual curiosity took Cyriac of Ancona on travels to Athens and Epirus, and to Samothrace, where he saw the remains of the Temple of Neptune and marble reliefs 'with dances sculpted of Nymphs' – thus experiencing at first hand the facts of Greek civilization. Different voyages and other sorts of discovery were to be made by Columbus.

To some extent the two men loosely represent the two chief disciplines which might be called Platonic and Aristotelian in the Renaissance, the humanist-style scholar-cum-antiquarian and the man more concerned with the facts of the natural world. Religious and spiritual values were to be represented better at Florence; naturalism and rationalism better at Venice. Both were connected with advances in knowledge, and neither was independent of influence from the other. The

58. *The Pietà*. Botticelli

ethical Neo-Platonic climate of Florence, often deliberately unscientific and almost waywardly mystical, is artistically expressed at its finest by Botticelli [58]. All the sensuous naturalism of Venice, no less (indeed more?) Christian but less emotional, is summed up by Giovanni Bellini [59]. The two painters stand for their respective cities intellectually as well as artistically in the late years of the fifteenth century, and it is doubly right that Bellini should prelude later developments while Botticelli's standards expire virtually with the century.

By either route, whether mystical or scientific, man was harmonized into the universe, itself created by the greatest Artist. Metaphors of art rather than language seem indeed the best expression of the idea of cosmic harmony which lay at the base of Renaissance philosophy. Man has no need to feel wretched or disturbed; he has his place and his space in any concept, and has also the potentiality to create conditions for rising closer to God. Although most if not all Renaissance philosophy accepts the fact that we cannot understand God, we can learn to know him especially through symbols. Visible things remain images of the invisible world, but – and it is an important but – the symbols and images must themselves belong as far as possible in the realm of certitude, and indeed science. It is for this reason that Cardinal Nicholas of Cusa found the nearest adequate symbols for God in mathematics:

59. *The Coronation of the Virgin.* Giovanni Bellini

'most fixed and most certain' ('*firmissima atque certissima*').
Nicholas of Cusa is a much more truly 'Renaissance' figure
than Pico, but he has never attracted comparable attention.
His very biography is a typically international one: born in
1401 at Cues on the Moselle, partly trained at Padua, Papal
Legate in Germany, and dying finally at Todi in 1464. Italy
and the Papacy shaped him and gave him purpose, but he was
a Northern European and it was there that the most dramatic
events of his life occurred. Although buried in his titular
church at Rome, he had devised for himself a more practical
monument in the Hospital of St Nicholas founded at his
birthplace, and splendidly endowed by him. His mind was
much more daringly speculative than Pico's, and at the same
time he was perhaps less seduced by the sense of power given
by knowledge. His metaphysics led him to at least one concept that was to have relevance for later speculation about the

universe; he believed that the earth was not fixed but moving, although we do not notice it, and thus he became a precursor of Copernicus and Kepler. Some of his other beliefs, like the emphasis he placed on Christ as human God and divine man, seem to fit very well into the artistic climate of his period, and Masaccio's Trinity fresco in S. Maria Novella at Florence [71], for example, could be interpreted in terms of his philosophy; using throughout the science of mathematics, that composition makes, perhaps for the first time in Western art, credibly visible the invisible mystery of the Trinity.

Even where doctrine was not directly concerned, the humanists helped to dignify man's intellectual activities, turning the '*Studia Humanitatis*' into imitation as well as study of classical authors. They are schoolmasters rather than moral teachers, but concerned as much as Pico was to be with encouraging man's potentiality. Education comes from study of great authors of the past, and the language of the past is used for formulating modern ideas; a reflection of this is seen in Alberti's consistent reference to churches as 'temples', inevitably the word that Vitruvius had used. The ancients must have had knowledge of certain truths, artistic as well as theological – and it is in such a conviction that Alberti opens the prologue to his treatise on painting (finished, we know, on 17 July 1436).

With Leon Battista Alberti (1404–72) we encounter not only the ideal of the *uomo universale* and the humanist but also much of the humanity that remains typical of his century and its art. Although often since linked with Piero della Francesca, he was perhaps closer in temperament to such an artist as Mantegna, sharing with him serious knowledge of antiquity and a wish to re-create it (in Alberti's case manifested also by his comedy modelled on classical example) combined with deep concern for realism, dignity, and an ameliorative view of humanity. Though the author of treatises on architecture and sculpture, as well as painting, he was also the writer of an ethical educational dialogue *On the Family* and a lively mealtime discussion of the same nature, the *Cena Familiaris* where three of the Alberti brothers sit down to talk, providing sound instruction for their young nephews who are silent witnesses. It might have served to be painted as a sober, pedagogic symposium at the court of Mantua by Mantegna. The dialogue is typical of Alberti's precepts in its social rationality; it is essentially concerned with ordinary life, the avoidance especially of the dangerous pastime of gaming, and its conclusion is sane and *moyen sensuel* in its discreet, not too high-flown, moral: 'For every age and condition good habits are the ornament and splendour of existence.'

Alberti everywhere constantly refers back to an ideal of existence which is made splendid by the social virtues, and by an ethical rather than religious urge to be good and useful. Unlike some later art theorists he emphasized, for example, that painting attempts to please the multitude (*'tutta la moltitudine'*) – and he saw nothing wrong in that. Indeed, behind all his artistic instructions there is clearly present the standard of man, his needs and his legitimate pleasures. It was perhaps inevitable that Alberti should quote Protagoras for saying that man is the measure of all things. In his architectural treatise, *De re aedificatoria*, he takes a broad civic view of his subject, sketching – elaborating rather – the growth of a complete town from choice of site to the details of interior decoration in the citizens' houses: 'I am for having rooms particularly designed for virgins and young ladies . . . that their tender minds may pass the time in them with less regret and be as little weary of themselves as possible . . .'. It is not a matter just of isolated buildings for rulers or ecclesiastical purposes. The city becomes virtually a mirror of the harmoniously arranged universe, with all its buildings disposed according to their function, its planned spaces and ubiquitous sense of fitness in all its details. Alberti seems quite conscious of such cosmic parallels when, in his discussion on staircases, he notes that the best architects never put more than seven or nine steps together in a single flight: 'imitating, I suppose, the number either of the Planets or of the Heavens'. The ultimate purpose of the city is to provide the best possible setting in which the citizens can live, without dangerous ostentation: built through rational precepts for rational beings. The architect's purpose is to 'serve successfully and with dignity the needs of man'.

Alberti's own practice as an architect is inevitably rather disappointing, partly through the accidents of unfinished or altered work. He never had the opportunity to build the circular centralized church which he eloquently wrote about, still less to design a whole town. His own churches, like the Tempio at Rimini and S. Andrea at Mantua, are ambitious but eccentric and not totally harmonious edifices, with hints of a disturbed, disturbing element that preludes Mannerism. His ideals are better exemplified in the concept of Palazzo Rucellai [61]: town-house and palace for a prosperous Florentine merchant, the type of leading citizen in the community with whom Alberti must instinctively have felt most in sympathy. In his cosmic ideal city, there are three strata of society and architecture: the prince and public buildings, the poorer people decently housed, and the middle state of the wise, experienced, wealthy citizens who will occupy such homes as Palazzo Rucellai.

In the express belief that a town-house should be much more grave than a country villa, Alberti has designed a dignified and severe structure, speaking a new and entirely rational language. It has broken away from the plain dwelling or massive fortress-like Florentine palace, and replaced heavy rustication by graceful incising, hardly more than a suggestion of rustication which lightly patterns the whole façade in shallow regular relief. It is intensely sober against the exuberant but still carefully planned façade of a Venetian palace [60], which manages too to suggest a rich rather than sober interior. The Venetian façade is calculated in terms almost of drama, concentrating on big, central double windows, with clusters of balcony, and roundels of inlaid marble breaking the intervening areas of flat façade. At Venice the windows dominate. Alberti's windows are dwarfed by the single, new motif of the pilaster, applied regularly along each storey, varied by nothing except a different order of capital. Intellect rather than imagination has devised this logical (perhaps too restrictedly logical) result, typical of the mind which sought order everywhere and recommended gardens perfectly plotted in a symmetry found only in art, in the background of some fifteenth-century pictures where trees are neatly planted in even rows 'and answering to one another', as Alberti advised, 'exactly upon straight lines' [67]. It is from such ordering that harmony proceeds. The lucidity and sobriety which will characterize the occupant and his family are expressed in their house. Within, the rooms are to be sensibly disposed, well lit, with on the walls suitable paintings that themselves exercise an environmental influence. Nothing should be painted in the family's own rooms 'but the most beautiful and comely faces' which may influence the wife when she is pregnant and condition the beauty of her children.

When Alberti turned to the actual problems of painting, it was equally with rational and practical considerations in mind. It was typical of him as a humanist that he should write his treatise in Latin, and typically humane that he should translate it into the vernacular for the benefit of his friend Brunelleschi.

That in itself is a clue to the practical nature of the treatise which at the same time claims an important humanistic role for the artist. The art of painting 'contributes to the most honourable delights of the soul and to the dignified beauty

60. Palazzo Corner-Spinelli, Venice. Attributed to Mauro Coducci

of things'. Man's potential as artistic creator is stressed, with a simile that brings him close to the Creator: 'any master painter who sees his works adored will feel himself considered another god'. And the power of a work of art comes from its combination of beauty with truthfulness to reality, a truthfulness which Alberti believes can be established by following a set of rules. Selective observation rather than imagination is what he would encourage, but it is observation which is primarily concerned with man: mankind animates and gives value to a painting. 'The greatest work of the painter,' he writes, 'is the *istoria*', by which Alberti means a composition of figures united by a single, preferably antique, theme, of an emotionally charged nature. Painting is tacitly lifted out of being a mechanical craft, or having a merely decorative role; the painter is advised to associate with poets and orators, so that he may utilize their knowledge and learn from them since their art has much in common with his. The eloquence so much praised and sought after by the literary humanists is here transferred to a different category of creative activity: the painting, which at its best will prove so eloquently expressive that it will move the spectator to weep or laugh, depending on the picture's mood. The idea of a disturbed soul can be expressed in the face – a precept already embodied in Donatello's *St George*, incidentally, but exemplified for Alberti by Giotto's Navicella Fresco where he praises the Apostles' fear and amazement being conveyed by their gestures and expression.

What Alberti is really advocating is the painter's creation of a complete miniature cosmos; the figures of an *istoria* are to be set within a completely realized spatial envelope, projected on the picture plane through a knowledge of mathematics; the whole of Book One of his treatise is occupied with this necessary discipline, the science, as it were, which the painter must ally with art. Alberti would have been able to approve Jan van Eyck's Arnolfini group, painted two years before his treatise was written, because despite its merely empirical perspective and its lack of classical subject-matter, it possesses the copiousness and variety which he advocated; and among his list of suitable things to appear in pictures are 'small dogs'. The idea of the portrait appealed to him too, and in the closing passage of his treatise he asks only one – rather disarming – reward if he has been helpful to painters, that: 'they paint my face in their *istoria* in such a way that it seems pleasant . . .'. Once again, Mantegna comes to mind with his vivid assembly of the Gonzaga Court, and it is perhaps more than a happy chance that Alberti's portrait has been detected among the group who witness the Cardinal's return to Mantua.

Yet it is significant that Alberti wrote comparatively briefly on painting, in comparison with the ten books of his treatise on architecture: the necessary laws and truths of the universe, the mysteries of harmony and proportion, might all seem better, or more easily, expressed in buildings than in pictures. Even there man remains the standard – not only in the sense of creating and inhabiting what is built but in giving his proportions as the standard by which a harmonious building is judged. This concept derived directly from the classical source of Vitruvius and it found immediate response among all the Renaissance theorists. Vitruvius had described how the well-proportioned man with extended arms and legs fits into the perfect geometrical figures of the circle and square. And thus man really does seem at the centre of the universe. Luca Pacioli [62], the pupil of Piero della Francesca, and friend of Alberti and Leonardo, made a very typical statement when he said that in the human body were to be found all

62. *Luca Pacioli and a Pupil.* 'Jaco. Bar'

ratios and proportions 'by which God reveals the innermost secrets of nature'. In this way the framework of Christianity (very marked in Pacioli) is hastily built up round Vitruvius, but leaving man still the vital point of study, vaguely identified with nature and containing within himself the source of nature's secrets. What Vitruvius had described in words was easily translated into imagery, and obviously exercised great appeal.

Man is literally present behind the columns and church plans devised, for instance, by Francesco di Giorgio, one more practising painter-architect and theoretician. The capital of a pillar is shown by him almost metamorphosed into a living head – and it seems rather typical that he should have gone beyond drawing a mere schematized head, to produce instead an expressive physiognomy of a face that might be imprisoned in the stone. There is a certain haphazardness about his diagrams to illustrate Vitruvian theories

63. Vitruvian Man. Francesco di Giorgio

[63]; a graceful, somewhat wilting nude stands not quite four-square, to be contained within a circle, and yet, owing to his pose, not quite contained. One foot sticks out beyond the circumference, so that the demonstration has not properly worked. Leonardo's later, highly memorable, similar figure [64], with arms outstretched in crucified pose, is dynamic and confident, master of the square and the circle which he seems to have conjured up round him. That is indeed an arresting symbol of man his own moulder; but it is ideal where Francesco di Giorgio's youth is merely human, caught in a pose that suggests someone stretching in faint weariness.

Vitruvian man might lie embedded in architectural diagrams and plans; by his physical proportions he might be directly related to a building. And a real man might experience a sense of being one with the cosmos, raised as high as Pico thought he could go in the material world, when he entered a church like S. Maria delle Carceri at Prato [65], a synthesis of

64. Vitruvian Man. Leonardo da Vinci

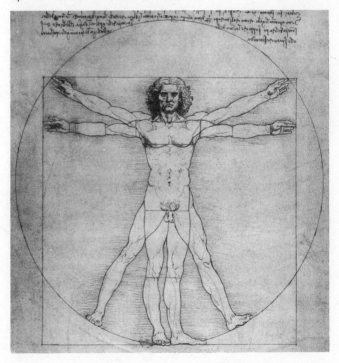

Vitruvius and Christianity: in plan a circle within a square, enclosed within a Greek cross. Its exterior is compact, patently formal in its planning, and highly concentrated. It might almost have been designed to express Renaissance rebuttal of the Gothic tendency to meander; the eye perceives and enjoys the certainty of its presence and the area in which it is circumscribed: 'A Gothic building cannot simply stop, it has to fade away.' (Henderson, *Gothic*.) Its interior [66] is all compact dignity, conscious restraint, lucidity and order. Art is not expressed in richness or mystery; the plan of the building is not gradually apparent, traced slowly by the eye, but is immediately comprehended, a spacious circle of brightness, marked at intervals by the contrasting verticals of dark *pietra serena* and arched over by a dome. The ground-plans of Vitruvian theory have here taken on three-dimensional

65. S. Maria delle Carceri (exterior), Prato. Giuliano da Sangallo

66. S. Maria delle Carceri (interior)

actuality; a man might stand at the centre of this temple and almost feel himself expanding to touch the rectangles of the walls, aspiring towards the perfect heaven expressed by the floating dome that springs from them, itself seeming to hold at its heart the white radiance of eternity.

Such art clearly states its aim: to express the fundamental cosmic truths of proportion, order, and harmony which lie under external appearances. Hence the necessity for restraint which Alberti particularly emphasized. Richness of ornament, carving, gilding – the artistic fancies which then still largely fascinated Northern Europe – are likely to be disastrous, mere additional factors which militate against true beauty: 'a certain regular harmony of all parts of a thing' – as Alberti defines it in his architectural treatise – 'of such a kind that nothing could be added or taken away or altered without making it less pleasing'. Art thus, in a sense, opposes life; it is one instead of multifarious; its concern is the pursuit of beauty rather than nature. In Alberti's garden the trees, we have seen, must be planted in regular rows [67] – advice of the sort usually, and wrongly, associated with the eighteenth century. But what Pope was to miss in the too patently plotted and regimented grounds of Timon's Villa, 'No artful wildness to perplex the scene' is exactly what Alberti and many of his contemporaries were trying to avoid. Wildness

67. *Garden of Love*. Attributed to the school of Antonio Vivarini

and perplexity are qualities of ordinary life which should be banished from art. In place of the real Renaissance Italian town – crowded, noisy, with narrow streets, still half-medieval – is the ideal town which haunted several artists' imaginations and which is embodied in a perspective picture associated with Piero della Francesca [68]. That this is at Urbino today is symbolically correct, because its place is in

68. *An Ideal Townscape*. Circle of Piero della Francesca

the circle formed about Piero, Alberti, Laurana, and Francesco di Giorgio, and it crystallizes all those aspirations to civic-cosmic order which could never be carried out quite so perfectly in any real town – not even at Pienza [33].

Although the painting was possibly executed to serve as some realization of the antique stage settings described by Vitruvius, it is more closely connected with Alberti's projects. It is, as it were, an entirely modernized Florence, with several variations on Palazzo Rucellai enclosing a spacious piazza at the centre of which stands on a platform a circular building, temple rather than church. Untidy actuality has been replaced by this silent, unpopulated city which combines harmonious restraint with variety (each palace being differently designed). Art has put the world we know into order and made us perceive the truth of things; to reflect just the appearance of a known city would be to ignore the principle of beauty which lies in construction. In a view of the real world there are only too many things which, on the Albertian principle, would have to be removed before true dignity and harmony could become apparent.

Thus, by a paradox, there is more cosmic reality in the ideal townscape than in an entirely naturalistic one. Indeed, here the Renaissance once again parts from the medieval and Gothic world, suppressing vivid details in preference for the whole. No one could mistake the Urbino picture of an ideal city for an actual one; its conventions are quite obvious, the chief being the deliberate absence of citizens. Yet it is not at all inhuman – quite the contrary. It is a work of art which reflects entirely man-made works of art; in a way, its whole point is to show man's potentiality as a creator. There is no space here for Gothic delight in dark woods or flowery meadows. Nature in that sense of the word has been replaced, paved over by tessellated marble, swept away in the interests of beauty to make room for the mathematically proportioned structures of man, themselves with none of medieval individualism (Alberti specifically condemned the medieval town where each building was built in rivalry and without regard to its neighbour) but planned in careful relationship to each other and in a single harmonious style, as lucid as the atmosphere which surrounds them. This picture of them is equally carefully plotted: the circular temple at its centre, with lines of pavement leading the eye towards it, and the recession of the flanking façades which balance each other across the composition – a formal balance made yet more explicit by the complementary well-heads. If this is intended as a theatrical scene, it is ideally devised to be the setting where Renaissance men can act.

No other painter was to create such fitting actors for that kind of world as did Piero della Francesca. His art is the perfect blend of learning and humanity, formulating a complete cosmos inhabited by quite unidealized beings who yet are the centre of it. He built into his pictures a perspective structure which was architectural even when no buildings were utilized – and we hardly need the confirmation of his concern with the science of representation which is offered by his treatise on the subject, *De Prospectiva pingendi*. This is strictly practical and reveals no secrets of the painter's own aims; beyond the terms of geometry it refuses to be explicit – rather like his pictures. In Piero's work the Vitruvian human proportions of the column, which Francesco di Giorgio theoretically outlined, assume new meaning and validity. His men are ranged like columns, while his columns have an organic, living sense. There is no contrast between natural world and man, or man and his man-made environment. People stand rooted like trees, but are more permanent presences – eternal within the perspective tunnel that extends from the picture plane into the background. Existence in that environment presupposes dignity, because there is a place for every object. The whole structure is homogeneous; surface textures are barely differentiated, and everywhere there is restraint, intense control of technique, sobriety of costume, and a reliance instead on the importance of scientific art, perspective, anatomy, and proportion.

Nothing could well be less colourful and exotic than Piero's conception of the meeting between the Queen of Sheba and Solomon; and nothing could be more elaborately devised than the organization of *The Flagellation of Christ* [69] which has passed out of Passion 'illustration' into being a complex piece of formal pattern-making, in meaning still partly incomprehensible to us. The picture seems to retain its locked-up secret, even while appearing at first glance to be all openness and lucidity. It is *about* several things, we may guess, and one of them is certainly order or harmony in a strictly mathematical sense. Those are the sort of laws in which Piero della Francesca believed; he neglected topical actuality to achieve a timelessness which only adds poignancy

to his depiction of Christian scenes. The planning of space and interval in *The Flagellation* is all related to the incident which remains emotionally but not literally at the centre of the composition. Piero's sophisticated science and deliberate emotional control result in a painting of Christ's Passion as effective as any more disturbed, more realistically presented scene. It invests with dignity even the moment of being tortured – and extends this envelope of the dignified to judge and torturers, as well as to Christ. The incident is preserved in a perfect cube of atmospheric crystal, framed by the patterned ceiling, supported by the receding floor of black and white tiles, in an element outside time [70]. No figure in the picture is smaller than Christ, but he is its keystone, its keynote, at the root of its proportions. Christ is the measure of all things; and his sufferings become no longer the incident of a moment but a fact of eternal validity.

In Piero della Francesca is summed up all the century's response to art that builds up a coherent world-picture, shaping a cosmos which is ultimately reassuring in its relation of man to eternity, and in its exploration of the eternity which is space. When not expressed in pure architecture, it could be expressed – as Piero's work reveals – in the architecture of pictures and in painted architecture. Stability and order of that kind, within the terms of Christianity, could inspire pictures which reject ordinary, as it were, mundane

69. *The Flagellation of Christ*. Piero della Francesca

70. *The Flagellation* (detail of 69)

71. *The Trinity*. Masaccio

realism just as much as does Piero's *Flagellation* and establish in its place the reality that art gives in obeying perspective laws. Thus God and man are harmonized already in Masaccio's Trinity fresco in S. Maria Novella [71] where the Crucifixion is realized under the painted barrel-vault of a completely simulated private chapel. At the base of the tall pilasters that frame the central group there is space for the kneeling donors; they share in the promise of eternity, raised above the tomb and the image of death which is stretched out below them. God's house becomes not a blaze of Gothic gold, but a logical structure, perspectively accurate, capable of being built (ready, in fact, to become three-dimensional actuality in Brunelleschi's buildings), solid-seeming, dignified, and true. There is no disparity between this architecture and the equally modern, fully characterized, solid appearance of the donors.

What is established is the cosmic hierarchy, which reaches inwards as well as upwards into the vaulted tunnel – an effect made vividly clear if the composition is reconstructed in cross-section. From the horizontal skeleton closest to us we move to the level of the kneeling donors, then to the slightly higher level of the Virgin and St John standing on either side of the Cross, which is supported by the hands of God the Father, himself placed on the highest, inmost level, impassively gazing out – the only figure seen in full frontal pose. The crucified Christ is the connecting link between lower and upper planes, between flesh and spirit, between the mutable world where man becomes dust and the immutable sphere which is God's. The composition ends with him, is closed by this figure which is not painted in any visionary way, but as solidly standing at the back of the chapel, literally supporting his Son.

The elaborately constructed perspective – so carefully planned that the lines of the vanishing points are still apparent, incised through the painted composition – demonstrates the truth of natural laws, anticipating Nicholas of Cusa's selection of mathematics as the most certain science, the one best fitted to stand as symbol of divine truth. In Masaccio the whole scene is harmonized by a sense of everything sharing the same nature. Gravity is at once the composition's mood and the controlling force which has disposed bodies in space. Carved and solid like the architecture, his people have the same plain tones, terracotta reds and greyish greens; the Madonna and the female donor might almost be the same

72. *Seven Sacraments* Triptych (central panel).
Rogier van der Weyden

person, so great is the affinity between them, but the pervasive feeling of certitude and harmony goes beyond that. It is as if geometry had proved the existence of God, and then humanity had become absorbed by the Godhead, itself partaking of human shape. In different terms, literary, more exalted, somewhat confused after Masaccio's sober clarity, Pico della Mirandola was to express this sense of ultimate unity: we have the power to raise ourselves to the concord existing in God's house, where 'we shall no longer be ourselves but shall become He Himself who made us'.

Inevitably, this is inflated compared to the more typical fifteenth-century view where God's humanity is stressed more often than man's divinity. The Crucifixion [72] is the central incident round which human beings are busily engaged in Rogier van der Weyden's Seven Sacraments Triptych, a Northern counterpart to Masaccio's fresco and, like that, startlingly original in its new presentation of a familiar theme. God's house is now a great church, luminous and spacious. The importance of light in a 'modern' church is emphasized by Felix Faber's praise of the huge church at Ulm – more beautiful than all others not through its painted or stone decorations but through its splendid light. Van der Weyden's is a sheltering fabric which stretches over the whole extent of existence. A new-born baby is baptized at the left; at the right an old man dies, anointed with Extreme Unction. Between these points, the church is animated by all the aspects of life: some people mere spectators, others engaged in the sacraments, and all placed in this God's-eye view of his own creation, where behind the huge Crucifix is seen the priest elevating the Host at Mass, expressing the continuing mediation between God and man. The sacraments themselves – those visible signs of invisible grace – are a metaphor equivalent to the arching church which provides the divine scaffolding for mundane existence. And the picture's cohesion is artistic as well as emotional; with its planned recession down the pillars, its airy coolness which harmonizes everything and illuminates the detail of the faces experiencing life, sometimes abstracted at a ceremony, or suddenly joyful – like the boys setting off after Confirmation [73]. The present, past, and future are all there; human life completes its course; other lives begin. Over it all Christ's Crucifixion continues to be eternal: a painful sacrifice, at which the mourning women for ever weep in agony, but a sacrifice which gives hope to humanity at every stage in existence.

Such pictures are using actuality for particular religious significance rather than for its own sake. The truths of the Christian religion gain a new dimension of truth by being set within the spatial world devised by a Masaccio or Rogier van der Weyden. The old ideas that the Renaissance emphasis on realistic elements in religious pictures confirmed its secular pleasure-seeking are not only too simple but actively wrong-headed – like Ruskin's belief that its architecture was pagan. Even the comparatively balanced and by no means imperceptive John Addington Symonds dismissed those pictures where contemporary Renaissance costumes and portraits were introduced as 'worthless to the student of religious art', and the presence there of architecture and landscape he called 'the usual padding of *quattrocento* pictures'.

But it is of course the whole point of such work that art and knowledge are not felt at the time to conflict with Christianity, testifying rather to the truths of it. Those luxury-living *quattrocento* pagans who so appealed to the Victorian imagination were really only themselves in doublet and hose, playing out an impossible tipsy pageant of the Renaissance devised from several sources – few of them authentic. Donatello, Rogier van der Weyden, or Alberti would have been amazed to see their practice and principles interpreted as licence of a kind hardly seen since Caligula's reign, combined with the donnish scepticism of intellectual circles in mid-nineteenth-century North Oxford.

The promised coming of Christ, the manifestation of God as man in the mundane world, was one of those subjects particularly which could unite all Renaissance concerns. Eternal and temporal meet when the Angel Gabriel salutes the Virgin Mary in her house at Nazareth; and in Renaissance art the angel does not come with any sense of supernatural shock but is solidly placed on the ground, a visitant half-expected, gracious in salutation and equally gracefully received by the Virgin. The room where the scene takes place is one that usually contains both participants – in place of the Gothic porch where, for example, Ghiberti's Virgin recoils before the onrush of the exotic, air-borne messenger. With Donatello [74] the mood is no longer one of dramatic contact and interaction of two spheres. There is nothing visionary in the angel's appearance, gracefully genuflecting in the

73. *Boys after Confirmation* (detail of left-hand panel of 72).
Studio of Rogier van der Weyden

74. *Annunciation Tabernacle* (detail). Donatello

richly decorated but shallow space, brought into such close *rapport* with the Virgin that each figure seems to throw awareness back on to the other: the angel reassuring and the Virgin timidly welcoming. Psychological, 'human' truth reinforces the Christian reality. The same intimate mood is less subtly echoed more than fifty years later by Benedetto da Maiano, whose virtuoso relief [75] elaborates the scene in the most typical way, opening up the space behind, and making the setting a coffered, decorated room, with vaulted colonnade beyond, extending into a garden perspective.

There the convention of harmonious architecture round

75. *The Annunciation.* Benedetto da Maiano

the very human figures, dignifying and enriching the scene, has perhaps reached its final use. For all its virtuosity, it has little sense of the novel. Fresh interpretations are needed, and the way is ready for a return to dramatic emphases; Lotto would show the Virgin's cat skeetering across the room in fright at the angel's manifestation, and Tintoretto would bring a thundercloud of attendant cherubs to stream through the half-ruined house and amaze the Virgin.

The standards of the Early Renaissance are better evoked by what sounds a typical composition of Masaccio's, now lost but described by Vasari, where the Annunciation was

made remarkable by a house full of columns 'beautifully drawn in perspective'. That is a piece of architectural painting which may be visualized in terms of Brunelleschi's actual practice – like the columns down the aisles of S. Spirito at Florence [76], receding in measured order, lucidly related to the wall area and clerestory above them, and leading the eye into a calmly spacious, utterly confident world. Something of the same effect, with architecture still Gothic in design, was attempted in *The Annunciation* [77] at Aix, painted *c.* 1444, perhaps by a French artist, where a particular meaning is intended by setting the scene in a church porch – symbolizing a prelude to Christianity. Though the porch is symbolic,

77. *The Annunciation* (detail).
The Master of the Aix Annunciation

it and the nave beyond are conveyed with all the perspective science the painter can command. They make up one more memorable metaphor of divine solidity and eternal truth, harmonious again rather than dramatic, the kneeling angel of the same substance as the kneeling Virgin. This is one aspect of Renaissance requirements that art should obey laws of nature and science.

78. *The Annunciation*. Konrad Witz

Another extreme, within the same terms, is represented by *The Annunciation* of Konrad Witz [78], painted about the same date. The banishment of detailed accessories, of genre elements, is here as absolute as the refusal to dignify by anything except the stark truth: a room of absolute bareness, a cell, but a cell which has touches of the madhouse rather than the cloister. Fra Angelico devised an *Annunciation* within an absolutely plain room, but his composition is ideal compared with Witz's determined actuality and shooting, faintly claustrophobic perspective of a plaster and lath room where the angel and the Virgin are – one is tempted to say – trapped.

But Witz's picture is the result of pondering on reality and
attempting to convey perhaps less the mathematical exactitude
of recession and more the sensation of it. His eye is almost
frightening in its unwinking intensity; *The Annunciation* is
harsh in its bare boards, crude timber, square of window – all
translating into visual terms the idea of humility and a life
about to be filled with purpose. Witz's truth to nature has
been likened to Pre-Raphaelite doctrine – but one great

79. *The Miraculous Draught of Fishes.* Konrad Witz

difference lies in the intention behind. The glassy transparent
water, shallow towards the pebbly shore, on which Witz
makes his Christ walk in *The Miraculous Draught of Fishes* [79]
only enhances our sense of a miracle – taking place not on
Galilee but at Geneva. It is all part of a common attitude
of mind, whether the expression of it is in dignified intellectual
terms or in ones consciously realistic and, quite literally, down
to earth.

The truth to which all Renaissance artists conform is a
cosmic one, and this is applicable even to painters like
Ghirlandaio who have been perhaps rather too uncritically

dismissed for their supposed gossipy genre quality. A very influential critic, Wölfflin, himself in need of being scrutinized more and respected less, pronounced on Ghirlandaio that 'he treats the content of his stories very lightly'. It is doubtful if this is true. There are certainly significant exceptions to it, and Ghirlandaio is probably closer to the heart of the Early Renaissance, both in its ideals and its expression, than Botticelli – whatever their respective merits as artists. More poignant than superficial is the blend of antiquity and Christianity (creating almost a painted equivalent to Virgil's

80. *The Death of St Francis.* Domenico Ghirlandaio

Fourth Eclogue) in Ghirlandaio's *Adoration of the Shepherds* (81], painted in 1485 as the altarpiece in the Sassetti family chapel in S. Trinita at Florence. There the frescoes on the walls around, treating of St Francis, patron saint of the commissioner, Francesco Sassetti, are impressive testimony to Ghirlandaio's serious artistic abilities. The monumental balance, relation of figures to architecture, and grasp of form in *The Death of St Francis* [80] look back to Giotto, from whom the composition derives, and forward to the High Renaissance and Raphael.

Just as Ghirlandaio may stand as the most characteristic painter of the period, so his patron Sassetti represents the typical emergent middle-class man: merchant and humanist, unlettered but fond of scholars and scholarship, interested in

81. *The Adoration of the Shepherds*. Domenico Ghirlandaio

antiquity but devoutly Catholic. His great-grandson described him as '*splendido, onorevole, e liberale*', and his chapel at S. Trinita is a monument to his qualities. The focal point of the altarpiece should be thought of in connexion with Ghirlandaio's lost fresco over the outside arch of the chapel, which showed the Tiburtine Sibyl revealing the birth of Christ to the Emperor Augustus. That prophecy from antiquity is confirmed by the event depicted in the altarpiece [81] and a further, novel synthesis of antique and Christian history is provided by the straw-filled sarcophagus in the Bethlehem stable. This is incised with a Latin inscription, carefully conforming to classical script, which reads: 'Fulvius, the auger of Pompey, slain at Jerusalem, said "the sarcophagus which covers me will give [to the world] the deity".' The unsurprising fact that no such Fulvius can be traced only adds a romantic air to the bogus inscription, testifying to the same urge that was contemporaneously leading Marsilio Ficino to seek literary syntheses of the antique past and Christian present. Indeed, it was probably another humanist scholar, the friend both of Sassetti and Ficino, Bartolomeo della Fonte, who conceived the inscription and perhaps directed Ghirlandaio in the subject-matter of the altarpiece and fresco over the arch. As a result, the past is brought to pay tribute to Christian truth, but that in turn gains subtly from pagan confirmation. It is in the same mood that Ficino established the immortality of the soul, pressing into service the evidence which could be gathered from every source, including 'the Persian wise men and . . . the Hermetic and Platonic philosophers'.

Artistically, too, Ghirlandaio's altarpiece represents a synthesis; to fifteenth-century eyes it was satisfactorily real, without any loss of dignity, organized but not schematized. It unites Italian idealizing tendencies with Northern vigorous genre elements – most clearly in the group of shepherds, directly borrowed from Hugo van der Goes's Portinari Altarpiece which had reached Florence ten years earlier. But the painting goes beyond being typical just of Florence; it is a perfect document in which the whole ethos of the Early Renaissance is summed up, and even its own middling merits are true to that. It evokes an atmosphere in which cosmic harmony seemed achievable, if not achieved, and truth something universal, available to all who searched diligently. It is a firmly human structure, solidly realized, with vistas extending in full daylight beyond the placid foreground group. And Ghirlandaio sees a procession of the world coming to worship – through the prominent triumphal arch, dedicated to Pompey, and symbol of classical antiquity – the God made man who lies at the centre of the picture and of the cosmos.

5
The Uses of Antiquity

While it is true that the Renaissance did not, strictly speaking, rediscover antiquity, its attitude to it, its steady invocation of it, and the uses it made of it all amount at least to redefinition if not rediscovery. Rome had always stood there as a symbol throughout medieval times – and for the Renaissance, too, classical antiquity was to be largely a matter of Rome – marvellous in its very ruins, mourned over already by Charlemagne's scholar, Alcuin, deserted by Pope and Emperor, a magical city which was almost a lesson in the vanity of even the highest human endeavours.

Very different was to be the attitude of someone like Brunelleschi, early in the fifteenth century surveying Rome and its ancient monuments with the experienced eye of a professional architect, looking to understand how these buildings had been constructed, what their proportions were, and the different orders of their columns, conscious the whole time that here were lessons to be learnt for modern art. At the end of the fourteenth century the Papacy had returned to Rome. Its re-establishment there was soon to be consolidated by the city's emergence as the capital again – no less than a minor renaissance – of the arts and culture. And what was fostered under Nicholas V, one more hero of Vespasiano da Bisticci's, was to bloom most splendidly under Julius II and Leo X. To Leo X, Raphael was to make his famous report on the antiquities of Rome. Brunelleschi's activities were quite unofficial, but also unprecedented. His wanderings with Donatello amid the neglected ruins of so much greatness, his burrowings in the past (which inevitably led to his being accused of treasure-seeking), and indefatigable attention to the detail of what he uncovered, are a symbol of the Renaissance which the period already appreciated. The first biography of him was possibly by a fellow-Florentine, Antonio Manetti – at least it was by someone who claimed to have known Brunelleschi. Manetti emphasizes the different style of Brunelleschi's architecture, derived from classical examples, when compared with what had until then been current. Only now were fully revealed the proportions of ancient buildings, the characteristics of Ionic, Doric, and Corinthian styles; the bad 'German' manner of architecture was soon replaced by the ancient-modern creations of Brunelleschi.

Strict examination of Brunelleschi's work shows that the massiveness of Imperial Roman architecture did not, probably, attract him at this time; and apart from his never-finished, somehow haunting, circular church of S. Maria degli Angeli, he never built a directly derived classical-style building. His greatest debt was to the native Romanesque architecture of Florence – represented for example by the church of S. Miniato – a style whose name betrays its own derivation; the pillars and arches which decorate the flat façade of S. Miniato are taken by Brunelleschi to become in their own three-dimensional right the graceful colonnade for the Foundling Hospital, the earliest Renaissance building. We may guess that in Roman monuments the problems of construction interested Brunelleschi at least as much as their style. Yet the Renaissance, as it flourished at any rate in Tuscany, wished to see Brunelleschi as the great innovator who returned to the achievements of antiquity. He became the artist-hero sketched already in the Manetti biography and finally consecrated by Vasari. Vasari added no new facts, but he silvered over with fresh eloquence Manetti's statements. Brunelleschi now comes like the new law, the new dispensation, sweeping away the barbarous Gothic style in general use, replacing it by good ancient architecture which was 'true'. So wide and deep was Brunelleschi's application, Vasari says, that he was able to reconstruct in his mind's eye the appearance of Rome before its fall.

As a concept, Rome and the world of classical antiquity meant exactly the same to the humanists and scholars. It offered the best possible truth; and the first step in appreciation of antiquity was to bring it out of a magical misty past (when the statue of Marcus Aurelius could pass as a brazen horse ridden by a man who might be Constantine or Theodoric) and realize that it had been a firm historical actuality. The shift from credulous awe to sober scrutiny is what typifies the Renaissance, separating it utterly from the attitude of, for example, Robert of Clari in the thirteenth century. He had been at Constantinople and described Sancta Sophia –

largely in terms of its rich silver ornaments and the many miracles worked there.

The Renaissance saw, perhaps also feared the implications of so seeing, the break between antiquity and Christianity. What came between the Renaissance and that classical past might be called barbarous, dark, or Gothic – but basically it was Christian. The sliding scale of the Renaissance, always in transition, wanted to go back before it went forward. It would recover the world which existed before Christianity, one it believed to be intensely moral as well as powerful, natural, and truthful, as witnessed by its monuments both artistic and literary.

What can be gained by study of the past was most eloquently and clearly expressed by the Florentine humanist Leonardo Bruni, whose *De Studiis et Litteris* was written just about the time Brunelleschi was probably carrying out his first personal excavations on the spot in Rome. It is interesting that Bruni's treatise is addressed to a woman, Battista di Montefeltro, among the first of a long line of scholarly Renaissance women. And it is particularly interesting that Bruni feels it necessary to defend the study of classical authors. In his day classical learning still needed protection: it had to be shown to be moral and virtuous – no less so than Christianity. The more this was demonstrated, incidentally, the more impressive must have seemed the antique world of philosophy and poetry which could achieve so much without Christ. And, even if no one openly said so, how much more truly admirable and moral must be classical antiquity compared with the behaviour of the chosen people as recounted in the Old Testament. Indeed, Bruni rather daringly pointed out that the Scriptures contain several stories which compare unfavourably with any treated by classical poets; and since such scriptural stories, unlike poetic ones, were true, he felt sometimes – he said – misgivings about them. The antique world of Greece and Rome told of man not in miraculous terms but in sober factual ones, with mankind alone in the cosmos and yet proudly capable of being good. The Renaissance was hungry for facts, and for reassurance; and both could best be supplied in combination by antiquity. Out of that study it would build new enduring monuments, in life, in literature, and in art. No wonder that the metaphor of building is soon in Bruni's mind. Latin is the foundation of study; and study is marked 'by a broad spirit, accurate scholarship, and careful attention to details'. It is the very sort of education that in practical terms Brunelleschi was contemporaneously giving himself. On that basis, Bruni says, an enduring edifice must be raised.

As for the edifice itself, its power is drawn from the subjects studied. For a woman one may dispense with Arithmetic, Geometry, Astronomy, and even Rhetoric. In their place there is, supremely, morals. Of course, Bruni mentions St Augustine in passing, but his pen quickens at the prospect of, as he explicitly says, not confining a woman to ecclesiastical writers. 'Morals, indeed, have been treated of by the noblest intellects of Greece and Rome. What they have left to us upon Continence, Temperance, Modesty, Justice, Courage, Greatness of Soul, demands your sincere respect.' That in itself might form an impressive enough code to live by. But it is supported by further study: of history (whence is drawn 'our store of examples of moral precept'), of oratory, where virtue is so warmly extolled and vice condemned, and of poetry. And here the most serious claims are made. In Bruni's view, the great poets of antiquity are essential to any education: 'For in their writings we find deep speculation upon Nature, and upon the Causes and Origins of things. . . .' Thus the closed perspective of a universe that ends in God – not really a true perspective but a vision – is exchanged for this long view down the corridors of speculation, in which poetic insight may prove as valuable in plain fact as divine inspiration.

But all this education takes on purpose only when one starts to construct comparable edifices. Bruni does not mean merely that education should help people live; it should help them create, giving them powers of expression. Bruni himself has achieved exactly this by writing the *De Studiis*, and Battista di Montefeltro took his advice. Several of her literary works survive; in middle age she was able to greet the arrival of the Emperor in Urbino by a Latin oration which was later printed. Thus the final result of study of the past is imitation – not lifeless copying but the imitation which is art in itself and also a bridge back, attaching the present to the great achievements of the past. Between those two worlds there is obviously no need for the Middle Ages; they are an interruption, an irrelevance, and, ultimately, an anachronism. A Gothic cathedral looks like a stranded dinosaur in the sandy waste separating the Roman temple from the modern temple-church devised by Alberti. Even the recent history of one's own land is irrelevant and not worth studying, at least when it concerns countries such as Bohemia and Hungary. That was the advice given to the young King of those countries by Aeneas Sylvius (later Pope Pius II), recommending instead Livy and Sallust as historians. In a tone which anticipates Miss Prism he added: 'Suetonius I exclude.'

The more the past was excavated, the truer – the more real – it became. Its bare bones took on not merely the marble flesh of antique sculpture but real flesh when a Roman girl's body was accidentally discovered in a tomb on the Appian Way in 1485. There are sufficient testimonies to early collectors of at least small classical objects dug up and taken away from Rome; in the mid twelfth century the Bishop of Winchester sent back to England some sculptures he had acquired there. But all this was sporadic. The lifetime of Ghiberti saw a marked acceleration of interest and knowledge, and his late art reflects an almost bewilderingly rich amount of antique prototypes, derived largely from sarcophagi. And Ghiberti has recorded in writing his sense of wonder at the chalcedony intaglio owned by the foremost collector of antiquities, Niccolo Niccoli. The *littérateur* and also collector, Poggio Bracciolino, wrote of the marvels of antique sculpture and bronzes, mute and lifeless, yet seeming to speak. What was needed next was some thrill of personal contact with living people from the past. All scholarly Italy was excited early in the fifteenth century when it was believed that the bones of Livy had been unearthed at Padua, but the discovery of 1485 was the most dramatic of all excavations.

Sometimes history provides a convenient event. It is convenient that in the High Renaissance Rome of the early sixteenth century the Laocoön sculpture group should be discovered, and it is conveniently symbolic of the simpler and more human fifteenth century that excitement should have been created around the first classical corpse to be discovered. Along with a majority of people in Rome, the humanist scholar Fonte went to see the exhibited body and reported on it to Francesco Sassetti, Ghirlandaio's patron. His letter was accompanied by a slightly amateur drawing, confirming how well preserved the mummified body was. 'This maiden,' Fonte wrote, 'who had lived when Rome had flourished was as shapely as she was noble.' The past was brought vividly to mind by the reappearance this time not of some statue but by the embalmed flesh of an actual Roman citizen, unknown yet still solidly present (her fingernails, Fonte noted, were firmly rooted). The shimmering haze peopled by mythical beings was replaced by actual physical fact; curiosity about what those Romans looked like was satisfied, agreeably too, since this one at least possessed beauty and nobility. Although the mummy itself was soon afterwards quietly reburied, its effect must have remained. Yet another perspective was given to the past – and not just to any portion but to the era which already fascinated the Renaissance exactly because it was so unlike it: a civilization which had existed and flourished before Christianity.

Other civilizations had existed without Christianity, but none had been so vast and powerful as the Roman Empire nor had left such impressive traces. Tradition, language, law are only a few of the things that bound Western Europe to those proud chariot wheels – so that even after its demise the Roman Empire still made conquests. With the addition of the adjective Holy, it was resurrected again as an historical phenomenon, vivid to Dante but faint to fifteenth-century Italy, an increasingly eccentric concept in Europe, which did not cease officially until 1806 when Francis II of Austria, the heir of Augustus, Trajan, Constantine, Frederick Barbarossa, and Charles V, abdicated and thus became the last of the Holy Roman Emperors.

Despite all the tributes paid to Roman literature and art, it was really Roman *imperium*, which impressed itself most strongly on the Renaissance; it was indeed inescapable, being deeply embedded in the very literature and art which the Renaissance admired. The myth of Greece was comparatively slow in establishing itself, and its empire has remained to most people one of intellect rather than geography. If one compares the ethos of two somewhat comparable plays, *Coriolanus* and *Timon of Athens*, the Renaissance response and lack of response to two antique worlds is vividly contrasted. Though as famous a figure as Alcibiades passes briefly through *Timon*, the Athenian world stirs no particular associations in Shakespeare's mind and clearly means very little to him. But Rome stands for cosmic inevitability, a world force against which the individual will pit himself in vain, with the results seen most tragically in *Antony and Cleopatra* ('a Roman by a Roman/Valiantly vanquish'd'), but most patently and proudly expressed in the less sympathetic *Coriolanus*:

> . . . you may as well
> Strike at the heaven with your staves as lift them
> Against the Roman state, whose course will on
> The way it takes, cracking ten thousand curbs.

Here is a harsh and heavy world of political fact, whose lessons were very clearly spelled out by Machiavelli. Those Roman emperors, he calmly noted, who were averse to severe measures failed to control either the legions or the ordinary people, and their own ruin inevitably followed. This is one of his observations in *The Prince*. In his treatise on Livy's history he is yet franker and more shrewd; he mentions the all-too-peaceful attitude of Christianity, idealizing the sufferer and his pain, which makes Italians slavish and weak. With that he deliberately contrasts pagan times and the action of sacrifice 'full of blood and ferocity'. It may have been terrible but it gave character to the people who witnessed it. Much more of a true historian than someone like Bruni, Machiavelli is inevitably much more 'realistic'. He cannot suppose that the past is merely a series of moral *exempla* which will lead us to practise modesty, continence, and justice. Radically different were his deductions. And it is not surprising that his reading of history, combined with his knowledge of men suggested that the prince will often find himself needing to violate the laws of charity, religion, and humanity.

Thus many of those great men of the past who stirred Renaissance imaginations did so through the power, usually the military power, that they had exercised. The world evoked by Alexander, Hannibal, Scipio, Julius Caesar was heroic but aggressive; even their moments of magnanimity were effective partly because they came from world-conquering figures and were frankly unexpected. Those Roman triumphal arches, whose design Alberti was eager to incorporate in his church façades, were expressions of the crushing might of the State; they were intended to impress not delight, and indeed their forms remain heavy, artistically uninspired, mighty but monstrous. They were raised to strange gods, human beings deified, immortalized by dedicatory inscriptions which have ensured that the names of the emperors Titus and Septimius Severus shall never be forgotten.

The stern yet triumphant echoes of such ancient, imperial assertions were caught and made to resound most superbly by Mantegna. While architecture and sculpture could take hints from classical monuments, only in painting or in literature could there be re-created the extent of that antique civilization, whose mystique is still powerful today. All that Mantegna felt is crystallized perhaps when one pauses in modern Rome, half-marvelling, half-moved, at the sight of the modern drain-covers stamped with the eternal initials S.P.Q.R. That Mantegna responded to the concept of antiquity often already in ruins only increases the sense of awe which he conveys. If he mourns, it is more stoically than the Middle Ages but with a deeper sense of what a marvellous world – *Mirabilia Romae* – was brutally destroyed. Even in ruins it retains its greatness.

This mood is shared by the extraordinary and involved Renaissance-antique allegorizing novel, the *Hypnerotomachia Poliphili* (dated 1467 but not published until 1499). Perhaps the book's title was a deliberately pagan answer to the intensely Christian *Psychomachia* of the fourth-century poet Prudentius – the first Western example of a purely allegorical poem. The *Hypnerotomachia* is one of the first examples of antique prose pastiche, breathing confused respect for love, ancient sacrificial rites, hieroglyphics, and herms [82] – and ancient architecture. The hero Poliphilus visits the ruined city of Polyandrion, with its temple of Pluto: 'worthy monument of things great in the eyes of posterity'. Just so does Mantegna place a fragment 'of marble foot, sole remaining portion of

82. A Triple-Headed Herm. Woodcut

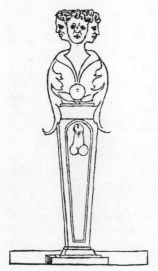

156

a classical statue, beside the living foot of St Sebastian in a picture of his martyrdom (in the Louvre). It serves as poignant reminder of an artistically splendid culture – rejected by the Saint, product of it, and a favoured member of the Praetorian Guard. Splendid but pitiless is the ultimate effect; against a richly ornamented Corinthian pillar the saint is tightly bound, cruelly tortured and bleeding from Roman arrows. There might almost be some moral ambiguity in the scene, for Mantegna's response to antiquity seems here as strong as his reaction to the Christianity which will destroy it.

At Padua, where Mantegna trained and worked in his early years, there was a university deeply marked with a serious tradition of classical scholarship, and a revival particularly of Latin letters. Mantegna's own master Squarcione was a collector of antique bric-à-brac. The city was the site too of Donatello's Equestrian Monument of Gattamelata [83], that Renaissance answer to the classical challenge of the statue of Marcus Aurelius, and itself thoroughly military and Roman in its celebration of a victorious commander. Padua was to prove a naturally sympathetic climate for the rustic antiquity evoked by Riccio's small bronzes, while its more learned academic attitude to the past was artistically summed up early in the sixteenth century by Riccio's fully Roman

83. Equestrian Monument of Gattamelata. Donatello

bas-reliefs for the tomb of the famous physician Girolamo della Torre who had lectured at Padua. A much earlier teacher at Padua, Vergerius, strikes the severe, even harsh, note which is typical of Mantegna's view of antiquity. For the son of the Lord of Padua, Vergerius wrote an important treatise (*De ingenuis moribus*) which exercised considerable influence throughout the fifteenth century, though written about 1392 – just at the very period when the medals of this ruling House were reproducing Roman imperial coins. Vergerius's treatise is masculine, aristocratic, and martial in its tenor. It expects a prince to be more perhaps in the mould of a Gattamelata than an Augustus. The training of a boy in Arms is as much a liberal art as training in Letters; and ultimately Vergerius, having named the Spartans and Scipio and Alexander, turns to his addressee's own family for 'notable instances of warlike skill'.

More than his well-known series of the *Triumph of Julius Caesar*, it is Mantegna's Eremitani frescoes (now barely surviving in the bombed church at Padua) which fully state his preoccupation with the antique world. There once again it is a setting of cold stone and marvellously carved, polished marble which builds up an impenetrable, unpitying framework for an ordeal; high walls of utter hardness against which a Christian martyr may beat in vain. Not accidentally can one think of these pictures in sculptural terms, for Mantegna executed some sculpture. Now it is St James who alone, except for his guard of Roman soldiers, stony, impassive men, scarcely living forms of metal and leather armour, moves through this triumphant architecture which is the visible expression of hostility to his religion and to himself. When Pater spoke of a Botticelli Madonna as one of those 'neither for Jehovah nor for His enemies' he deduced her indifference perhaps rather wantonly. But the phrase has some real aptness before the spectacle of Mantegna's frescoes, where the artist seems resolved not to commit himself but dispassionately to depict – yet with all the evocative power of his art – the clash between new religion and antique world. Though the spiritual victory may be Christianity's, visually it is antiquity which triumphs.

Unlike Brunelleschi, Mantegna had not examined the nature of Roman concrete, nor the exact proportions of actual surviving buildings in the city. As far as we know, he had not visited Rome when he painted these scenes, and he hardly needed to. It was an idea of antiquity which he possessed, more intense than any reality and more hallucinatory and exact in its detail. Brunelleschi's homage to the ancients was connected with their knowledge, but Mantegna responds to the prestige of the Roman State, manifested by its buildings which seem immutable. These monuments of marble and brass, now concentrated cones and spirals of sheer solid masonry and now massive, decorated structures, are instinct with man's power to create. They speak the same severe high language as the people who inhabit them – among whom St James is the intruder and the victim. They are essentially soldiers' buildings. A huge triumphal arch forms a wall in the judgment hall where the Saint is sentenced; he pauses in a street on his way to death [84], and the great bulk of building

84. *St James on his way to Martyrdom.* Andrea Mantegna

behind him bears a bas-relief of armour hoisted in victorious procession. Everything in this antique world is hard and clear and firm. Nothing will bend or change the judge's sentence, inflexible as the verticals and horizontals of the architecture, against which echo only the thin sharp lines of lances and swords. There is no space here for pity. Martyrdom is no glorious moment, but the brutal dispatch of a trussed, recumbent body in a stony landscape where the vegetation is as petrified as the buildings, and the martial onlookers betray no more emotion than does the owl perched high up on a bare branch which grows from a classical ruin.

Gazing innocently at these compositions, we might think they had been painted to drive home – as painfully as an arrow in the flesh – the dangers of opposition to the Roman State, 'whose course will on . . .'. The man who sets himself against that inevitable power will end as a corpse in a ditch, and the helpless St James, lying awaiting death, has already been robbed of human dignity, a horizontal bundle in a landscape of noble verticals, upright monuments, and proudly monumental men. Mantegna is a historian not an ethical teacher. No more than Machiavelli does he soften the facts of the past; he is uncommitted about the goodness of antiquity, content to show it – with all the skill at his command – as having been great.

Few artists at any period have achieved such remorseless intensity in evoking the past. Mantegna's severe consistency might almost have been the object of Reynolds's dictum, actually prompted by Poussin, who remains the only painter with whom he can be paralleled: '. . . when such subjects of antiquity are represented, nothing in the picture ought to remind us of modern times'. But that rigid eighteenth-century neo-classic doctrine is different from the generally much more humane concern of the Renaissance with antiquity. It looked at antiquity to learn – which is not quite the same thing as copying. It saw a spacious world, natural and yet organized, in which moved natural, dignified men and in which had been created natural, realistic, and yet marvellous works of art. Perhaps every period is haunted by the myth of an earlier golden age – or perhaps the Early Renaissance was the first period fully to have this sophisticated awareness. Certainly its goal was not the Garden of Eden; it was a city rather than a garden – any location, in fact, which had been man-made and was inhabited by man. It is by the standard of man that everything should be judged. To the humanist scholars Cicero was the great teacher, *magister vitae*, who gave a code by which a good life can be led. To the artists, Vitruvius was equally a great teacher, *magister artis* one might say. Cicero's rules of conduct are paralleled by Vitruvian rules of art. Such things can be established, even down to the correct proportions for the relationship of each feature to the next in the human body, and Alberti's treatise *De Statua* conveniently codified the results in a practical table he recommended to sculptors. The whole position is summed up towards the end of the fifteenth century by a humanist scholar who was also interested in the arts, Rudolf Agricola. Educated at Cologne and Pavia, polished by a stay at the Este Court in Ferrara, settling eventually at Heidelberg where he died prematurely, Agricola is one more international figure, the product of a Northern as well as Southern environment. Writing to a friend on his course of studies, he recommends not only the ethical teaching of the ancient philosophers and historians, as Bruni had done at the beginning of the century, but also ancient authorities on architecture, painting, and sculpture. 'These arts . . .,' he goes on, 'do not belong exactly to that part of knowledge which explores the essence of things, but they are related to it. . . .'

If 'modern' Renaissance artifacts borrowed from past achievements, it was partly to develop on the same lines, to be able to claim that they too were related to the 'essence of things'. They would be *true* as the antique monuments were; like them, they would be an admixture of nature and idealization. Sculpture, for instance, had a natural origin – so Alberti claimed – but the sculptor did not just follow nature; he selected and fused different aspects of nature, in the interests of harmony. Alberti's table of proportions in the human body was thus the result of a general law adduced from a wide number of examples. This type of classicism was really to be more significant than the actual illustration of scenes from antiquity, revival of antique forms, or even talk about churches as temples. And by the early sixteenth century, new ideas of harmony and idealization were to find, for example, the horse ridden by Donatello's Gattamelata too minutely realistic. Such a criticism is highly significant; but it could come only after the first lesson from antiquity – its truthfulness – had been learnt.

In sculpture this inevitably concerned the human body.

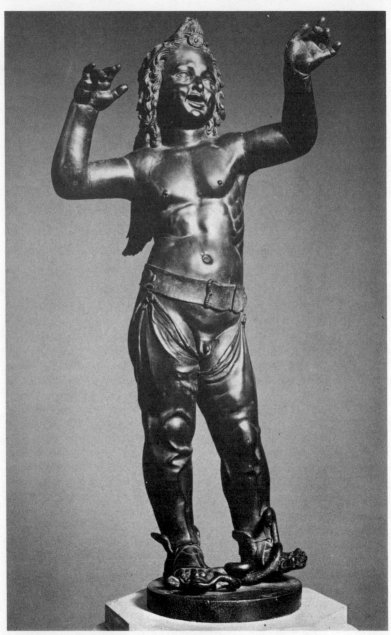

85. *'Cupid-Atys'*. Donatello

Quite apart from the design, therefore, it was an achievement which recalled Classical antiquity – and nothing since – when Donatello produced the first free-standing life-size bronze statues. His so-called '*Cupid-Atys*' [85] actually passed as an antique in the seventeenth century, and it remains the most remarkable sculptural essay into a pagan ethos before Riccio's small bronzes. But it is also a remarkable study of a child's body, the proportions of which are now seen, in contra-distinction to medieval ideas, to be not merely those of a miniature adult. The subject was one of interest to the Renaissance – which was to make of children a favourite artistic theme [86] – and Pomponius Gauricus (author of the *De Scultura*, of 1504, which criticized Donatello's horse) disarmingly said that he would have written about the matter 'if my sister had a child'. Antique examples might prompt an interest, but nature was still seen to be essential.

Although the intended significance of Donatello's '*Cupid-Atys*' may be baffling, as is the occasion of its production and

86. *Boy with Bagpipes*. Andrea della Robbia

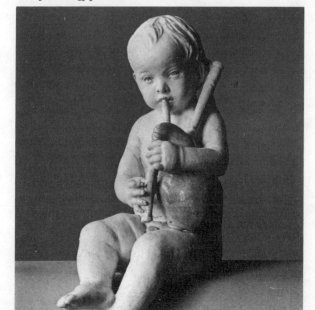

its commissioner, the statue suggests an attitude to antiquity just as serious as the attitude to nature. Part of its baffling quality comes from its assembly of classical motifs, wings and tufted tail, and winged sandals, hints of infant Bacchus blending into hints of Mercury, all shot through with erotic energy. It does not appear to copy any individual antique, paying tribute rather to the impact of antiquity on a modern consciousness. And part of its marvellous natural quality is the sense of movement: freedom expressed in the upraised arms and especially in the face where bronze holds the mobility of a fleeting, excited emotion, creasing the cheeks, opening the mouth. It captures a very real force, sexual, wild, and almost dangerously exuberant; even though it is most unlikely that the boy originally held a bow and arrow, there is a certain aptness in the suggestion that he could do damage. Amid the truth to nature, the exquisite finishing of detail, the surface vitality and cheerful vivacity, lurks a disturbing psychological truth – ultimately typical of nothing except its creator. The Renaissance was not full of comparable work, although it did produce some other mysterious and even disconcerting recollections of antiquity. Much more truly typical is the charming, ever-popular *Putto Holding a Dolphin* [87], executed by Verrocchio as a fountain figure for the Medici Villa at Careggi. This presents no problems and speaks the almost Rococo language of the boudoir-antique. Where Donatello's boy seems drunk with unholy glee, Verrocchio's is smiling in slight breathlessness – a gracefully poised, playful, innocent child, very much as adults like to think of children.

Perhaps it is too summary a judgment to find Donatello's statue the product of imagination, Verrocchio's of fancy – yet there is some substance in the definition. Certainly Verrocchio's winged boy is ruler of a wide kingdom of Renaissance fancy, one already adumbrated in medieval times, where antiquity is a half-fairy place, with Paris and Helen and Orpheus dressed in fashionable clothes, sophisticated courtiers in an amorous climate. Chaucer's Cupid in the *Legend of Good Women*, gilt-haired, wearing an embroidered silk tunic and a wreath of roses, is part May-King, part mythological personage. This charade mood, with antiquity only an excuse for pageantry and light-hearted love, was easily transferred into pictorial decorative terms. This is the antiquity of wedding-chests and other painted furniture [88], where the subject-matter may be classical but it is not felt

87. *Putto Holding a Dolphin.* Andrea Verrocchio

88. *The Rape of Helen.* Follower of Fra Angelico

89. *Aristotle and Phyllis.* The Master of the Housebook

90. *The Boyhood of Cicero*. Vincenzo Foppa

incongruous that the characters should wear modern dress – with results that may be just decorative, witty, or unexpectedly poignant.

The Master of the Housebook, handling his novel dry-point medium with sophistication, produced a late-fifteenth-century Aristotle and Phyllis obviously without any sense of incongruity [89]. Indeed, he probably thought that contemporary dress sharpened his anti-feminine little moral: a woman can make a fool of even the greatest philosopher.

It is with very different effect that Foppa portrays the youthful Cicero, whose fifteenth-century costume for long concealed the fact that it is he [90]. This fresco was probably part of a didactic cycle in a palace at Milan, where the Virtues or the Liberal Arts may have been personified, each accompanied by an historical representative. Cicero's application as a schoolboy, mentioned in Plutarch's biography of him, is touchingly suggested by Foppa's placing him in a miniature study where he props himself up, concentrating on a book.

A room of firmly planned horizontals and verticals, classically plain and harmonious yet with pleasing niches and embrasures, all suitably small-scale for its youthful occupant (as Alberti might have advocated), is constructed round this figure who meant so much to Renaissance scholars, from Petrarch onwards. Foppa's boy could be the ideal pupil of a Vittorino da Feltre: improving his mind at an early age, surrounded by books but sensibly at an open window, and led by natural inclination to enjoy scholarship. The lesson to be drawn by the spectator is obvious; it is not merely the importance of education that is stressed, but active self-education – Cicero is not being taught. The example chosen is historical and true. Not the childhood of Christ, nor the infancy of Hercules, is the theme. Between religion and mythology, the Renaissance cleared a space – the most significant space – for ethics, and that is really the subject of what may be called *The Boyhood of Cicero*.

But though mythology went on serving a variety of decorative purposes [91/92], often diluted into charming works of art not intended to be taken too seriously, Donatello's '*Cupid-Atys*' reveals that antique mythology could exert a

91. The Martelli Mirror

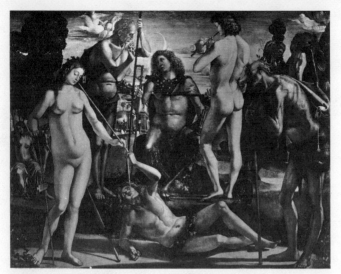

93. *Pan*. Luca Signorelli

spell as intense as history's. It could take on too an ethical
motive, inherited from medieval love of allegorizing, concerned with inner rather than outward actions, and revolving
round the life of the soul. Although there may be naïvety
in some of the extreme forms of this, such interpretation is at
least closer to the origin of mythology than the nineteenth-
century view that the gods were natural phenomena personified. The allegorizing of mythology not only tended to
obscurity in itself, but was positively encouraged by a
hermeticism associated particularly with Neo-Platonism at
Florence. The idea of 'secrets' – in art as in religion – seems
to have obsessed people outside that circle; Dürer hoped to
get some secrets from Jacopo de' Barbari, and even Raphael
looked to the elderly architect Fra Giocondo to teach him
'*qualche bel segreto*'. Perhaps a mystery is intended to lie at the
heart of Donatello's statue, reserved always for initiates and
now difficult to recover.

Such is probably true of another great work of art, now
physically lost to us, destroyed in the Second World War,
Signorelli's *Pan* [93]. This was painted in Florence for
Lorenzo de' Medici and almost certainly was not an illustration of any specific classical text. It does more than revive

170

antiquity; it interprets it, and produces a pagan *conversazione* which has all the moral weight of a *sacra conversazione*. Even the most prosaic art historians were stirred to a sort of eloquence at the sight of this picture, with its sense of melancholy and music, and its proudly enthroned, shaggy god of nature. Perhaps the germ of the picture lies in the Homeric Hymn to Pan which evokes him at evening when Echo calls from a mountain-top, and the nymphs sing to him of his father Hermes. A picture like this explains why the nineteenth century tended to see antiquity as the motivating force behind the whole Renaissance. There is something primeval and eternally classic in Signorelli's mysterious male and female nudes clustered about their god at twilight, banished creatures of mythology who had always existed and who have now crept back in the welcoming Renaissance air. Indeed, Signorelli's female nude – calmly and completely naked – heralds the

94. *Eve*. Antonio Rizzo

triumph of Venus in Renaissance art: a triumph of the flesh often expressed by Eve, no less assured of herself in Rizzo's statue [94], despite a conventional pudic gesture.

Whatever its exact significance, Signorelli's *Pan* represents a new category of picture, a category associated above all with Botticelli. *The Birth of Venus* and the *Primavera* are now so famous that it may seem surprising how rapidly Vasari passes over them – and he is almost the last person to mention them for three hundred years. But Botticelli's antique world is private and personal; his very technique is less 'Renaissance' than Signorelli's. His people with their printless feet barely possess substance enough to bend the meadow grass on which they walk, and unlike the harsh, modelled nudes of the *Pan* they cast no more than conventional shadows. Against the naturalism of that picture, Botticelli's *Pallas and a Centaur* [95] is deliberately insubstantial, a sophisticated and allusive allegory where antiquity and Medici symbols (the interlocked rings decorating Pallas's robe) combine in unique effect. Yet it is right to think in terms of the artist's response to antiquity, because Botticelli's delicate antennae picked up the most subtle of all vibrations. The classical world is lost to us and can be recovered not through archaeology (nor study of Vitruvius), still less by direct imitation of ancient forms, but only through the imagination. Although it is true that Renaissance Italy contained few pagans, one likely non-believer – who came to Florence, was patronized by the Medici and was actually painted by Botticelli – was the Greek soldier-poet Marullo. His poems, especially his *Hymni Naturales*, might well have suggested ideas to Botticelli, a hypothesis strengthened by Marullo's admiration for Lucretius, for there is something very Lucretian in some of Botticelli's imagery.

Perhaps Botticelli's Centaur's head is, as has been suggested, derived from classical sculpture. It hardly matters, because his Pallas is a quite frankly un-classical goddess – if indeed she *is* Pallas and not a personification of some virtue – and the subject is probably of fifteenth-century devising, with ethical significance. The Centaur may stand for the bodily passions, brutish, dumb, but biddable. A familiar creature, though never before treated with such importance, a centaur occurs in pictures of St Anthony Abbot; it directed the Saint on his journey across the desert, pointing the way because it could not speak. In Botticelli's picture it is more puzzled than

95. *Pallas and a Centaur.* Botticelli

rebellious; Pallas's fingers clasp its curling forelock, and at that touch it seems to recognize a superior will.

The painting has the calm, allegorical inevitability of a masque – and just the same artistic relation to reality. Pallas does not need that large yet property spear; long flowing hair conceals, as it follows, the curves of her shield; and the springing wiry sprays of myrtle or olive that wreath her arms and crown her head seem to embody the tender, pacific mood with which a goddess has infused the whole scene. Marullo wrote a hymn to Pallas ('*sapientiaque eadem et quies*') but it is also of an English poet that one thinks here: 'She strikes a universal peace through sea and land.' Milton's vividly pictorial imagination is always producing lines and phrases that recall Botticelli, and it is less absurd than it might at first seem to make some comparison between them. Intensely Christian, they both can evoke an antique world the more poignant for its artificiality; the same type of conscious classicizing which could turn Edward King into a Sicilian shepherd is apparent in Botticelli's imagery which is highly refined and exquisitely wrought, a playing upon associations which argues a literate, highly refined circle of patronage.

Although it is usual to remark on Gothic elements in Botticelli's art, if only its dependence on wonderful linear rhythms, he is in some ways more *avant-garde* than *retardataire*. Not just the emotion that so violently shakes his late religious pictures lifts him into the late-sixteenth-century style of Mannerism, but what can only be called the filigree-work of his mythologies where art evolves from artifice. His antiquity does not synthesize with Christianity, because he is too sophisticated. Whether or not moral *exempla* lie under such pictures as the *Pallas and a Centaur* is unimportant. Largely lacking in sense of three-dimensional weight, it lacks moral weight also. It is no more convincing in that sense than is the moral of *Comus*. But like *Comus* it has another sort of conviction which continues to give it validity. Unrealistic, unscientific, unmoral, uninstructive about the facts of the past, flying – and that most gracefully – in the face of all the teachings of Alberti and the artistic aspirations of the majority of fifteenth-century artists, it rests its validity on a highly sophisticated proposition: that it is art.

In the years that followed, indeed already in the late years of the century in which the picture was painted, Botticelli's art must have increasingly seemed no art at all. We may be sure that it was losing relevance, since the artist's reputation became rapidly obscured and lay for long in the dark. It might almost seem as if antiquity had led him into a cultivated cul-de-sac. Ghirlandaio might be commonplace, but at least his solid plain humanity offered some basis on which new and more eloquent structures could be built. Donatello, Pollaiuolo, Signorelli, could all offer examples of the human body studied naked and in action. Mantegna inculcated a serious attitude to the historical past.

Such artists would have their relevance for Dürer, Raphael, Michelangelo. Those are mere random names to suggest the rising tide of new attitudes and new ambitions which were soon to make the achievements of the Early Renaissance look rather tentative. Even the tremendous, excited respect it had manifested for antiquity would come to seem rather naïve. What it had really discovered that mattered most was nature. It is in truth to nature, said Leonardo, that the painter is superior to the poet. Leonardo showed virtually no interest in antiquity, but what he was to uncover about nature had its relevance far beyond artistic circles. Born in the middle of the fifteenth century, only a very few years younger than Botticelli, he built a bridge not backward but forward, carrying the Renaissance into the stormy noon brilliance of the next century.

96. *The Virgin of the Rocks*. Leonardo da Vinci

6
New Earth and New Heaven

Much that the Early Renaissance had striven for, and a good deal it had hardly guessed at, is crystallized in Leonardo's *The Virgin of the Rocks* [96]. Art and science, faith and reason, are marvellously married there to make a work of art with quite new and astonishing impact. Its realism positively eclipses reality. Its nature is so natural that most other fifteenth-century pictures look stiff and contrived beside it, dry against its liquid atmosphere, harsh against its subtly muted light. And its ambition is tremendous. Its creator is not content with the portrait, not interested in *virtù*, indifferent to classical antiquity, unconcerned here with Vitruvian proportions and architectural perspective. That '*omniparente natura*' which Cyriac of Ancona found captured in a painting of Rogier van der Weyden's is here re-scrutinized, re-captured, and finally challenged. Leonardo has become a *magus* of the kind Pico della Mirandola described, who weds earth and heaven by magic, bringing into the open miracles concealed in the recesses of the world. After such a creative act, art could not be the same again. And it is, of course, right to see in Leonardo da Vinci the initiator of the grand manner of the High Renaissance.

Yet the intensely firm, marvellously natural-seeming structure which is *The Virgin of the Rocks* only temporarily synthesizes the forces of faith and reason, soon to pull apart again and shake the whole Renaissance edifice. Leonardo initiates the High Renaissance, but he also foreshadows its dissolution. A heavy if splendid burden had been placed on man; were he to falter, the whole fabric would begin to topple. The sureness of Van Eyck's Arnolfini couple in their room, the *prontezza* of Donatello's *St George*, such are the qualities to be consecrated and heroically enhanced by the High Renaissance temple of art – which might be thought of in terms of some Roman building of Bramante's, symbolizing the volume of the cosmos which harmoniously surrounds the central, dominant figure of ideal man. But Leonardo is in himself a disturbingly uncertain magician, an increasingly wayward power, seldom able to fuse his genius into actual creativity; and in *The Virgin of the Rocks* there perhaps already lurks some ambiguity and unease. After all the aspiration towards harmonious proportion, Bacon was to pronounce that there is 'no excellent beauty that hath not some strangeness in the proportion'. Donatello had allowed a tremor to pass over the features of St George, without disturbing the statue's basic sense of harmony; in Michelangelo's later sculpture the figures toss as if in torture.

Pico della Mirandola's optimistic beliefs in the *Oration on the Dignity of Man* echo strangely in a world which with Luther denied man's free will, with Montaigne was sceptical of knowledge, and with Donne could celebrate the glorious irrationality of Christianity as virtual proof that it is true. Even the nobly human Christ of the fifteenth century – Masaccio's, Van der Weyden's – crucified without loss of dignity, shrinks to become Donne's paradox of inward divinity but outer wretchedness: 'that worm and no man, ingloriously traduced as a conjurer, ingloriously apprehended as a thief, ingloriously executed as a traitor'.

After that apostrophe it is hardly surprising that ordinary men would lose the allure of their physical envelope. The solidly natural, innately dignified *quattrocento* human being is raised temporarily to High Renaissance godhead (never better enshrined than in the triumphant scale and spirit of Michelangelo's *David*) and then retreats to become a wavering, insubstantial creature, flaming mysteriously across El Greco's pictures but present as early as Pontormo's, and vividly evoked by Chapman's verse:

> Man is a torch, borne in the wind, a dream
> But of a shadow . . .

There were to be painful aspects too of the artist's autonomy, concurrent with a realization that nature and the cosmos may prove more hostile than harmonious. Leonardo wrote proudly of the sense of being alone, but for Pontormo it had become an unexhilarating awareness of sheer loneliness. He was to be, though only briefly, Leonardo's pupil. Something that is veiled in *The Virgin of the Rocks* has become quite patent in Pontormo's disturbed, disturbing altarpiece in the church of S. Michele Visdomini at Florence (set up within Leonardo's lifetime), a picture nowadays recognized as a decisive crack in the always somewhat contrived High Renaissance edifice of heroic certainties.

As well as gathering up the aspirations of the fifteenth century in which the major portion of his life was spent, Leonardo's art contains all these potentialities. The story which Vasari tells about one of his earliest pictures – a head of the Medusa – may not be true in every detail but it propagates a new sort of myth about a work of art, and well suggests the new sort of artist which Leonardo was to become. Leonardo's *Medusa* was an *invenzione*, a subject of his own devising, prompted probably by the shield-like shape of a piece of wood which his father had brought to be painted. For the mythological monster Leonardo assembled and studied real insects and reptiles: art is based on detailed, loving scrutiny of nature, in this instance prolonged to the point where the artist – so Vasari says – did not notice the smell of the dead creatures. It is the scientific application we expect of Stubbs working on the anatomy of a horse, but scarcely of a painter devising a fabulous Gorgon. When it was finished, Leonardo placed it in an empty room to dramatically confront his father who drew back terrified. Vasari includes in his account Leonardo's arrangement of the window, to make the light dim. It seems not excessive to detect even here that sensitivity to atmospheric effects, preference for subtle tones of muted brilliance, as at evening, which the *Notebooks* emphasize and recommend to painters. Like another Diogenes, the typical *quattrocento* artist had gone about with a lantern, illuminating every corner of his composition in the desire for certainty. Leonardo's first act is to replace that unnatural clarity by a diffused luminosity, substituting what might be called 'soft-edge' painting for the sharp angles and hard corners of earlier constructions.

Such moderated light will lend charm, Leonardo wrote, to every kind of face. By this new standard it is not what is known to be there that is painted, but only what is seen. Charm lies in the softness and vagueness, and 'charm' itself, with its useful double meaning of spell and attractiveness, seems a new quality to be desired in art, passed on from Leonardo to Giorgione and then to Correggio.

The diffused light planned to bathe the *Medusa* was to increase not its charm but its mysterious verisimilitude. The mistaking of a picture for reality is a time-honoured legend, literary tribute to a famous artist's skill, but something more emerges from Vasari's story of Leonardo's picture. Not only did it drastically disturb the first spectator, but this effect was exactly Leonardo's intention. '*Questa opera serva per quel che ella è fatta,*' Vasari makes Leonardo say. ('This work serves its purpose . . . .') This is rather different from anything Alberti would have encouraged. He certainly thought of pictures as affecting the spectator, but not as serving to frighten him. Dürer, so easily paralleled, yet not always convincingly, with Leonardo, stated that the two purposes of painting were to further religion and portray people. Even when Leonardo might seem to accept those precepts, as in *The Virgin of the Rocks* or the *Mona Lisa*, he yet brings something of a Medusa touch to them, a disturbing and faintly disassociated air which makes the spectator draw back for a moment, as Leonardo's father had done. There is something uncanny in their very realism. Art no longer provides an agreeable reflection of the known world, superior to our experience chiefly by being ordered and planned in the interests of higher harmonic truths, but now shakes us by presenting something never before seen, horrific in its impact, and momentarily upsetting our grasp on the real world. That Leonardo perpetrated this trick of art – merely the first of several frights he ingeniously devised – on his own father is something that hints towards a climate of sharper psychological concern, one in which Dürer, like Leonardo, would think it worth while noting down a particular dream.

The Virgin of the Rocks has nothing of the forceful shock intended by the *Medusa* but much of the hallucinatory power of a dream. For all its astounding realism, it remains a vision. Even its significance is partly mysterious – as mysterious as its setting. Perhaps Leonardo was encouraged towards the eventual concept by legends in the Apocryphal Gospels of Christ's infancy: a mention of the youthful St John the Baptist miraculously hidden in a cave at the Massacre of the Innocents, watched over by an angel, and the meeting of the two holy children on the return from Egypt. Perhaps the emphasis laid by the angel on St John is explicable by the picture originating in a Florentine commission, since he is the city's patron saint, and it may even have been begun as the altarpiece which Leonardo was officially commissioned to execute for a chapel in the Signoria there.

It is thus quite likely that Leonardo started with a typical *quattrocento* task, to provide an altarpiece of conventional subject-matter. But at each step he achieves new and indeed quite startling effects, constantly defining by the light of nature every aspect of his picture. It is as if he went on asking himself what would be most natural, regardless of the conflicting realities of divine persons and physical setting. For theological purposes St Thomas Aquinas had defined the borders of faith, which is assent to revelation, and knowledge, which is assent to something proved by reason. There is all the difference between believing and perceiving, though he had recognized a difficult area where the natural and supernatural, reason and faith, tend to overlap. Leonardo begins at that point; his composition is a symbol of how far nature can carry conviction, even in the bodying forth of the supernatural. His whole life was devoted to the principle of looking with the aid of reason, trying to disregard the pressures of faith. When discussing, suitably enough, the function of the eye, he noted how it had been defined by countless writers: 'but I find by experience it acts in another [way]'.

The same deliberately empirical attitude lies behind *The Virgin of the Rocks*. A wish to get to the heart of nature and know her secrets was perhaps Leonardo's main impetus in everything he did; and such interest as he had in painting might almost have been to set up rivals to nature, fusing all his knowledge of her into the creation of things super-natural. In *The Virgin of the Rocks* the laws are nature's but the final creation Leonardo's. And he here defines the natural in many ways that cut across previous artistic assumptions. The result is organic rather than intellectual. Other painters threw a deliberate schema over nature, seeing it in terms of conscious mingling, enriched by art, whereby buildings were allied to scenery, minor groups of figures enlivened background spaces, and objects were artistically rearranged to mirror a cosmic order. This showed the artist's invention. Alberti wrote of a delightful artificial grotto he had seen, an almost eighteenth-century construction of varied stones and shells, but Leonardo designs a grotto which is the more marvellous for seeming not human work at all. It appears the product of natural forces: the rocks ribbed and smoothed by the constant motion of water, present in the winding river but felt in the subaqueous light and as giving moisture for the plants – each recorded with botanical accuracy – that grow so thickly and yet are pallid.

It still seems a region untrodden by man, because the

figures who kneel in the grotto have something of the same inevitable growing quality as the plants; they are no stranger than their setting, and there is no sense of their incongruity within it. Organized into being one group, their different actions are all harmonized as if into a single action – expressed by the triad of hands: the angel's dominant pointing one fixed midway between the Virgin's arching above and the Infant's blessing below. Thus the actual 'subject' becomes complex not simple; it is the consecration of the Baptist, the revelation of the Infant's divinity, and probably the Virgin's recognition of her Son's destiny. None of this is narrated in the usual manner of *quattrocento* pictures, but in a more natural way – suitably for the astounding naturalism of the protagonists. All splendour of dress, brightness of haloes, is dispensed with. The sacredness of these figures is itself almost organic, as if evolved from within like the thousand cells of paint which form the nearly palpitating surface of their flesh, the tingling electric texture of their curled hair. So much sense of reality in a picture is disturbing and becomes supernatural. It has quite ceased to have the daylight realism of Ghirlandaio, or the mathematical certainty of Piero della Francesca. Leonardo is hovering on the brink of another sort of truth: that there is no single aspect of reality, no certainty at the heart of nature, but only flux.

The more living the beings that Leonardo created the more subject they are to natural law; their marvellously blooming flesh and bright hair can decay and fade, and it is hardly too fanciful to detect mortality already present in the dark cave of *The Virgin of the Rocks*, just as Pater saw in Leonardo's depiction of the Medusa head 'the fascination of corruption'. The shadowy figures retain their secret; the angel becomes almost a Sphinx in pose; and the misty background hints at change, as the solidity of rock recedes in aerial perspective into insubstantial cloud shapes. It is as if nature will finally triumph in the swirling river, which will wear away the rocks and reclaim the grotto, bringing the world back to its primal state before God divided the waters.

It is mystery that separates the ethos of the *Mona Lisa* [97] from the assured and tremendously factual portraiture of the fifteenth century. Her realism is not a matter of surfaces but of depth – and it is not surprising that this has often been felt to be disturbing. Confident, humane, plain people – whether bent to their task [98], or in death as homely as

97. *Mona Lisa.* Leonardo da Vinci

98. Pulpit-Bearer. Anton Pilgram

in life [99], or sophisticated yet straightforward like Rossellino's marble *Bust of a Woman* [100] – are replaced by this idol swathed in veils, receding from us even while she sits there, elusive and untouchable. This is not so much what a person physically looks like as an attempt to convey in paint the impression of a personality. If the mark of the High Renaissance were just confidence then Rossellino's *Bust of a Woman* would be of the High Renaissance, for it is as confident as delicate. It is a living image, but an unmysterious one –

99. Tombstone of Bishop Donato Medîci. Antonio Rossellino (?)

easily in *rapport* with the spectator, despite its sidelong gaze and pupil-less eyes. Its quality is rather that so highly praised by the fifteenth century: of *vivacità*. It seems ready to speak, quick to observe, itself the product of careful observation to the point where every bodice hook and lace is transferred into marble. In fact, even to modern eyes distracted by its costume and fashion, it remains recognizably the portrait of a woman one could know. Its achievement consists in transferring into the marble medium the very vitality of ordinary existence

100. Bust of a Woman (Marietta Strozzi?). Antonio Rossellino

but giving it a permanent air. Art thus defies mortality, and this bust shall live to show what the sitter was like when the actual woman is dead.

No one could think Leonardo's woman the living image of Mona Lisa (if indeed it is she and not some other person, older and perhaps a widow). One can sense the intended gap between actuality and art. Art is no longer concerned with mirroring the sitter's features and appearance in objective fashion; but adds as it were the artist's image in the mirror

101. *Self-Portrait*. Albrecht Dürer

too, overlaying outward nature by inner, more wayward nature which moulds the face and the whole atmosphere as it has moulded the clothes, softening them out of contemporary cut into timeless draperies. Dürer had already shown, with different effect, how much the artist mattered to himself [101]. Indeed, he was his own Mona Lisa, absorbed in his own uniqueness, eternally fascinated by his own features, grace of his clasped hands, the ripple of his long, curled hair. What are mountains of lunar mystery in Leonardo's portrait are in

Dürer's recognizably the Alps, which he had successfully crossed, and then recrossed on his return home.

If art history worked the way most art historians like to think, the *Mona Lisa* would have suggested a great deal to Dürer; not only did he almost certainly never see it, but his portrait has priority. And though he asserts himself so proudly in it, he was not to remain unaware of those sensations, thoughts, even touches of weakness, which have made Mona Lisa's eyelids 'a little weary'. When Dürer watched his mother die it was with reluctant fascination: 'I saw also how death smote her two great strokes to the heart. . . .' And, most frightening of all, he observed the shift of her expression at the moment before death; with intense poignancy he notes 'she saw something dreadful'. A later self-portrait drawing of himself shows him stripped of all finery, a naked, sick man who points to the portion of his body where there is pain. When he experienced his apocalyptic dream it was of rushing waters that fell from heaven; not merely did he wake and lie there trembling, as people have always woken from nightmares, but he thought it worthwhile to record his sensations in words and by a drawing. Dürer's conclusions may not be as personally disturbing as Hamlet's, but they are more far-reaching. He detects something rotten in the state of the universe.

Although so much Early Renaissance art – painting, sculpture, architecture – had polished a perfect mirror to reflect the interlocked cosmos of solid earth in harmony with bright heaven, with mankind at its centre holding the key, nature kept spotting and breathing on the glass. Man was not always noble and proud, but utterly commonplace – just a peasant setting off for market with his wife, as Schongauer depicted them [102]. Seen through the misleading perspective of history, Schongauer's engraving looks hardly revolutionary; but quietly it makes a claim for the most ordinary scenes of everyday life to appear in art. It stands at the beginning of a chain, soon to be substantially added to by Dürer and Lucas van Leyden, which culminates with the underestimated etchings of Adriaen van Ostade in the seventeenth century: there too the themes of poverty, country life, daily tasks, are treated with a tender gravity and Spartan respect. And Pico della Mirandola's man the moulder of himself has shrunk to a hunched peasant on a rustic bridge, trailing his fishing-line in a stream at evening.

103. *The Nativity at Night*. Attributed to Geertgen tot Sint Jans

Nature itself, in the sense of landscape and atmosphere, was soon to be a subject for art to study. Leonardo's grotto would come to serve as virtually sufficient purpose for a picture; in different ways Giorgione and Altdorfer were to release nature from being merely something set around mankind, and allow its forces to reign without the aid of men. The miracle of the Incarnation was to be expressed not only in the pagan-Christian synthesis proposed by Ghirlandaio, but in more truly 'natural' terms by the contemporary *Nativity at Night*

[103], close in style to Geertgen tot Sint Jans. Only the Infant
and the angel appearing to the shepherds provide illumina-
tion in the darkness – and a sort of proto-scientific realism
attempts to suggest light falling on the bare hill-side and light
radiating out, as if from a lantern, from the divine Child who
is born to lighten mankind's darkness. Rightly, his brightness
shines up fully into the Virgin's face but only brushes with a
faint glow the face of St Joseph who stands apart. What is
here attempted, and indeed beautifully achieved, was to be
elaborated and set out by Leonardo in his concept of a night-
piece with a fire, vividly described but never painted by him.
Just as much as Leonardo, but with simple empiricism, the
painter of *The Nativity at Night* incorporates experience into
art; his subject remains one of the most traditional and

104. Scene from *Le Livre du Cuer d'Amours Espris*

popular of all religious subjects, but his treatment of it is
virtually novel. And even where high fantasy and medieval
romance provided the subject-matter, atmospheric truths to
nature could give new reality to allegorical fiction. Though
Botticelli's might have seemed the style in which to illustrate
King René's *Le Livre du Cuer d'Amours Espris*, the unknown
artist realized the scenes with a poetic response to shadowy
rooms and twilit landscapes [104] which remains extraordinary. This painter too instinctively anticipated the precepts of

Leonardo; he too knew how glowing embers can teach light to counterfeit a gloom.

Closely examined, the cosmos is strange, and even the clear matter-of-fact account in Genesis of God creating the world – which Michelangelo was to make epic – can become the uneasy evolution seen by Bosch: a greyish, watery dream of things heaving and coming to life, disturbing the surface by suggestions of horror. It might almost be a malign creator, instead of the great Artist and Architect, who set these creatures in motion. And elsewhere Bosch did play the malign

105. *The Garden of Delights* (detail). Hieronymus Bosch

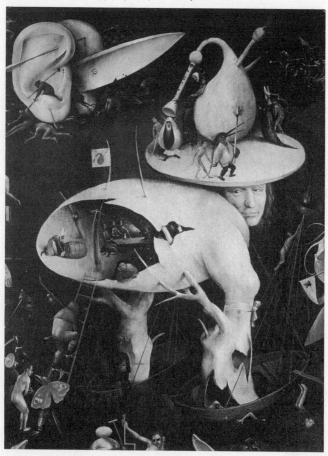

god [105], creating monsters never conceived before: clock-work beings, with wheels and jewels, as if constructed by a diabolical watchmaker, spiky fruits which are carnivorous, birds with hands and butterfly wings, and animals who turn into musical instruments. The cosmos is jarred; mankind is at the mercy of things often grotesquely beautiful, delicately painted mechanisms who stalk the world with insane confidence. Mantegna's Sea-Monsters [106] are antique noblemen, intensely human in their pugnacity, beside Bosch's nimble, lethal, and utterly un-natural creatures – too far removed

106. *Battle of Sea-Monsters*. Andrea Mantegna

from our consciousness to have normal emotions, and obeying the mad laws of their own world where a human ear or an exploding egg may lie about the landscape. Dürer and Leonardo did not even dream of such determined irrationality; art has broken the mirror of the ordered universe and put it together again in what seems wanton perversity. But perhaps that very perversity is true to the depths of human nature.

Bosch is probably the most extreme reminder that fresh examination of man and man's potentialities could produce disconcerting results, even while being fully art. Indeed, no other painter of grotesque fantasies (not even Bruegel) has the delicacy of touch which makes Bosch's cosmos so crystalline: sphere within sphere of glass inside which half-transparent creatures gyrate and gambol, hard as glass too, a goldfish-bowl which becomes a symbol of the human mind. New awareness – however disturbing – is what art like his wants to incorporate within itself. And it is noticeable how beautifully observed are natural phenomena in his pictures, fantasy never disdaining a scientific precision in atmosphere and landscape which aids their final Surrealistic effect. Bosch's scenes are patently unlike our own normal experience – but then so is the scene of *The Virgin of the Rocks*. On reflection, it is less surprising than it might at first seem that Bosch and Leonardo were close contemporaries.

If Bosch, and to some extent Leonardo also, dig down to reveal new depths in man, other artists would raise him up, taking him out of the environment in which he seemed naturally rooted and creating him on the scale of a demi-god. It is still prosaic humanity who gossip and attend, somewhat perfunctorily, in Perugino's *Christ Giving the Keys to St Peter* [107]; and for all the symmetrically disposed architectural setting, the marble space is like a playground, with noisy, distracting, subsidiary incidents. Raphael's *Betrothal of the Virgin* [108] by comparison speaks the new and utterly confident language of ideal forms: ideal setting – with a quintessentially lucid temple, not built by hands, a vast

107. *Christ Giving the Keys to St Peter*. Pietro Perugino

structure compacted of air and light, all voids and echoing space, its centre a luminous empty doorway – and ideal figures who move, if they move at all, with *adagio* rhythm. Even the dramatic incident of a disappointed suitor snapping his rod has become an exercise in sheer, static grace, the testing of sinewy stick against supple knee, performed without effort by someone whose balance is perfect enough for him to remain calmly suspended on one foot during the action. A *quattrocento* angel, never mind man, usually kept both feet on the ground; but Raphael's youthful suitor is given angelic grace, and gracefully integrated into the composition so that his action seems – to the untutored eye – part of the rhythmic ritual instead of protest against it. With great suavity, but quite openly, nature is defied – or, in a pun, is deified. Raphael's scene is as much an extreme as is a typical picture by Bosch – merely, it moves in the other direction, taking us up away from the stubborn humanity of Piero della Francesca, the more gossipy detail of Perugino, into a perfect sphere of such altitude that ordinary beings can breathe there only with difficulty.

Harmony rules in a way that to the average fifteenth-century spectator would probably have seemed too passion-less, robbing the picture of that lifelikeness the more prized for having been so recently captured. Leonardo had made his people inhabitants of an environment more mysterious than any we know; Raphael gives his a superhuman clarity and grace in a universe of Euclidean certainties; and Michelangelo – who was to become the god of the new century's idolatry – makes even grief harmonious in the ideal group of the *Pietà* [109]. There the Madonna's face retains virginal youth and an unemotional expression; Christ's body is polished, unmarked marble, graceful in death, fluid amid the richly flowing clothes of the Madonna, themselves wrinkled in virtuoso melody at her neck and sweeping in great folds to the ground. In this elevated language of almost Cornelian sentiment, a single gesture is sufficient to command attention; the Madonna's hand is extended expressive of sorrow but serving also to display her burden. Her grief is public and seems to enlist an audience to witness it – while retaining a decorum which forbids any emotional excess. Wölfflin found 'unsurpassed pathos' in Christ's dead body, but Michel-angelo's group avoids all such extremes of feeling. Previously, sculptors and painters (such as Ercole Roberti) had made the subject one of extreme pathos and stark grief; in Northern sculpture, particularly, Christ's body was often an angular, gaunt corpse stretched stiffly across the knees of a woman whose sorrow had made her equally gaunt. Michelangelo's Christ is not dead but sleeps; at least, his body suggests the glorification of the Resurrection, just as the Madonna herself seems a miracle of youth. The effect of this *Pietà* is to make us wonder rather than grieve.

Never before had the subject been made so noble and heroic, positively forbidding the sort of identification which the *Quattrocento* had enjoyed in its art. Michelangelo begins with the most unnatural concept of mother and son, concentrating rather on the idea that his group should depict divine natures, not subject to mere human stress, age, or physical weakness. The Madonna is a goddess, Artemis rather than Mary, remote, even imperious, a marvel of carved draperies – thin dress and thicker robe – who holds on her knees an exhausted athlete, with gleaming body and graceful limbs. The group is as much a vision as anything by Leonardo; art creates what nature has not, justifying itself by dealing with persons who were supernatural and who must therefore be shown true to that essence.

That climate can be chill for ordinary people if they continue to look in art for an extension of their own lives. And at all times the 'grand style' which such art represents has caused some difficulties; Reynolds was to emphasize its artificial character, and what he has to say is perhaps the most sensitive and attractive explanation ever given of it. But the style itself is a creation of High Renaissance Rome, developed in the sixteenth century and outside the scope of this book. What does both anticipate it and yet remain fully *quattrocento* in sympathy is the most 'natural' great art evolved during the fifteenth century: Giovanni Bellini's. In him Leonardo's scientific, speculative abilities are replaced by empathy, an empirical response to phenomena which is instinctively warm and light-loving. Leonardo is a hundred things apart from being a painter. Bellini is nothing but painter: all his knowledge is in his art, but it is none the less knowledge of a new kind, though not codified in theoretical writings, not shot through by any trace of scepticism – his being indeed perhaps the last utterly whole-hearted acceptance in art of the complete medieval-Christian structure before the shock of the Reformation.

110. The S. Giobbe Altarpiece. Giovanni Bellini

111. SS. Francis, John the Baptist, and Job (detail of 110)

Bellini's world is intensely stable, but naturally rather than intellectually or mathematically based. His faith is sure, and his reason quite effortlessly follows it. The Resurrection or the Transfiguration almost cease to be mysteries when set in luminous countryside – countryside which is not just background but the very texture of the picture, a garment of liquid light, with subtly coloured skies and soft brown hills, which flows round the figures. Heaven and earth are no longer two spheres, and it is without incongruity that the Coronation of the Virgin [59] takes place in the countryside around Pesaro. This *is* Bellini's heaven, with the fortress of Gadara lifting its towers on the wooded hill-side seen framed by the Lombardi-style throne: an open-air, country scene where four Saints solemnly gather to witness the intimate scene of coronation, simple not splendid, a tender almost rustic rite. Even the figures' nobility is – like their solidity – somehow natural. Nobody before Bellini had responded with such intensity to the poetry of the senses: the feel of sun-warmed marble, the look of a summer sky with drifting piles of cloud – a natural world where man is no intruder but neither is he an imposer of order. It grows and glows in its own way, never too wild, nor too tame. Beyond and around some marble parapet or carved balustrade, tribute to modern Renaissance art, there is always the palpitating atmospheric envelope of radiant air in which man stretches confidently, created by the play of shadow and slightly muted light, mellowing like a fruit in his natural environment.

The Coronation of the Virgin at Pesaro is only touched with what has become full Renaissance achievement in the S. Giobbe Altarpiece [110/111] – Bellini's contribution to that new heroic language, too easily presumed the creation solely of Leonardo, Michelangelo, and Raphael. The S. Giobbe picture is probably quite close in date to *The Virgin of the Rocks*, painted well before the end of the fifteenth century, and in its way it is no less seminal. The superb setting painted is an extension of its original architectural setting in the church of S. Giobbe at Venice: elaborate illusionism constructs this high-roofed chapel of marble and mosaic, filled by the composition of eleven figures, varied in type and generation and pose, but all magnificent. Renaissance interest in the human body – combined with a Leonardo-like meeting of opposites – provides the dialogue of age and youth between the dignified naked Job and the opulently naked St Sebastian. The picture's rapt mood – a harmony of celestial music, played by the seated angel trio – is extended outwards at the left by the proto-baroque St Francis who appealingly turns to include the spectator within the composition, one hand outstretched in a gesture anticipating Michelangelo's Madonna. The scene is neither earth nor heaven, but an ideal middle sphere, where even St Sebastian's martyrdom has left him almost unscathed. Everything speaks of conscious achievement: the saints physically impressive, deeply characterized as studious, devout, or fervent like the St Francis, all calmly confident, scarcely moving under the timeless spell of music played to them; and at the centre a tall throne with a cross mounted on a circle, like an emblem of eternity, holding the powerfully moulded Madonna, mother and queen, one hand upraised half-imperiously, the other clasping her Son.

There is no aspiration left, for everything is realized and achieved. Real and more than real, these ideal people are harmonized into their setting where art has carved and gilded an ideal chapel, luminous, soft-curving, an eye-deceiving edifice which is fit to stand as the Renaissance view of the cosmos: accessible and logical, created by a God who became man, the child on his mother's knee who is yet the central purpose of the universe, as he is of this picture. Splendour of the human body combines with splendour of architecture and costume, and to visual splendour is added the aural one of music, for which an honoured place is found at the Madonna's feet. The altarpiece format is itself a type of picture evolved by the Renaissance and it is here executed on huge scale, yet with no sense of the forbidding. Bellini's standard remains very much humanity's; there is nothing too astonishing, dramatic, or awe-inspiring in this balanced vision, with its poignant optimism, its gentle confidence, its deeply sensuous piety. When one despairs of explaining the Early Renaissance, it is sufficient to look at this picture where, with no premonition of a disturbing future, so many of its hopes and beliefs are given immortal expression.

Catalogue of Illustrations

The following are the chief abbreviations used:

Art Bull.: *The Art Bulletin*
Burl. Mag.: *The Burlington Magazine*
B.M. Cat.: *Catalogue of the British Museum*
J.W.C.I.: *Journal of the Warburg and Courtauld Institutes*
N.G. Cat.: *Sectional Catalogues of the National Gallery*, London
Pope-Hennessy, 1958: J. Pope-Hennessy, *Italian Renaissance Sculpture*, 1958

1. MAN LOOKING OUT OF A WINDOW. Plaster. *Paris, Musée des Monuments Français* (photo: Bulloz).
   A cast of one of the window sculptures on the façade of the Hôtel de Jacques Cœur at Bourges, 1443–53.
2. GOLDEN ROSE. Gold, 60 cms. *Paris, Musée de Cluny* (photo: Giraudon). Apparently the oldest extant example of a Golden Rose, given by Pope Clement V to the Prince-Bishop of Bâle early in the fourteenth century.
   Lit: Bunt, C. G. E., *The Goldsmiths of Italy*, 1926, 14.
3. PLANT STUDY. By Leonardo da Vinci, *c.* 1505–8. Red chalk on pink prepared paper, 15·5 × 16·2 cms. *Windsor, Royal Library* (reproduced by gracious permission of Her Majesty, Queen Elizabeth II).
   Lit: Popham, A. E., *The Drawings of Leonardo da Vinci*, 1947, No. 276.
4. SELF-PORTRAIT. By Ghiberti. Bronze. *Florence, Baptistery*. Detail of the framing of the left-hand of the so-called 'Gates of Paradise', completed in 1452.
   Lit: Krautheimer, R., *Lorenzo Ghiberti*, 1956, 9–10.
5. ST GEORGE. By Donatello, 1417. Marble, 209 cms. *Florence, Museo Nazionale* (photo: Brogi). The photograph shows the niche at Or San Michele with the original statue *in situ*; it is now replaced there by a copy.
   Lit: Janson, H. W., *The Sculpture of Donatello*, 1957, II, 23–32; Pope-Hennessy, 1958, 272–3.
6. THE MARRIAGE OF GIOVANNI (?) ARNOLFINI AND GIOVANNA CENAMI (?). By Jan van Eyck. Signed, 1434. Oil on panel, 81·8 × 59·7 cms. *London, National Gallery* (museum photo).
   Lit: Davies, M., *Early Netherlandish School*. (N.G. Cat.), 1955, 38–40.
7. HEAD OF ST GEORGE. Detail of pl. 5 (photo: Anderson).
8. PHILIPPE DE CROY. By Rogier van der Weyden, *c.* 1460. Oil on panel, 49 × 30 cms. *Antwerp, Musée Royal des Beaux-Arts* (photo: copyright A.C.L.). The right-hand half of a diptych, of which the other wing, showing the Virgin and Child, is in the Huntingdon Art Gallery at San Marino. Philippe de Croy (1431?–82) was one of the most distinguished of the cultured circle of the Dukes of Burgundy.
   Lit: Panofsky, E., *Early Netherlandish Painting*, 1953, I, 295–6.
9. MARCHESE GONZAGA WELCOMING HIS SON CARDINAL FRANCESCO. Fresco detail. By Andrea Mantegna. *Mantua, Castello* (photo: Anderson). See under pl. 10.

10. THE GONZAGA COURT. Fresco detail. By Andrea Mantegna. *Mantua, Castello* (photo: Anderson). The frescoes in the so-called '*Camera degli Sposi*' were completed by Mantegna in 1474. The return to Mantua of Cardinal Francesco Gonzaga took place in 1472. The date at which Mantegna began the frescoes is not known.
Lit: *Andrea Mantegna*, exhibition cat., Mantua, 1961, No. 26 (with bibliography).

11. THE STUDIOLO OF FEDERIGO DA MONTEFELTRO. *Urbino, Palazzo Ducale* (photo: Alinari). The view shows the elaborate *trompe l'œil* intarsia-work with cupboards which indicate the Duke's interests and pursuits. Above this level was originally placed the now-dispersed series of paintings of Famous Men and of the Liberal Arts. The ceiling bears the date 1476.
Lit: Rotondi, P., *Il Palazzo Ducale di Urbino*, 1950, *passim*, especially 337–56.

12. FEDERIGO DA MONTEFELTRO AND HIS SON. By Pedro Berruguete (?), *c.* 1477. Panel, 134×77 cms. *Urbino, Palazzo Ducale* (photo: Alinari). Not certainly by the Spanish painter, Berruguete, who is however recorded as working at the Court of Urbino from 1474 to 1478, along with the Fleming Joos van Wassenhove. Together they were employed on a scheme of pictures decorating the Duke's studiolo (pl. 11).
Lit: *Juste de Gand, Berruguete et la Cour d'Urbino*, exhibition cat., Ghent, 1957, 58–60.

13. STAIRCASE. By Mauro Coducci, *c.* 1498. *Venice, Scuola Grande di S. Giovanni Evangelista* (photo: Alinari). Coducci was made a member of the confraternity in 1498 and was soon after charged with the task of designing the staircase which leads up to the main *salone*.
Lit: Angelini, L., *Le Opere in Venezia di Mauro Codussi*, 1945, 66–71.

14. TRIUMPHAL ARCH OF KING ALFONSO OF ARAGON. *Naples, Castelnuovo* (photo: Alinari). The arch was begun under the impetus of the King's actual entry into Naples in 1443. Several sculptors were employed on it. Alfonso died in 1458 and the arch was in effect completed by 1466 – though some sculpture for it was never finished.
Lit: Pope-Hennessy, 1958, 330–31; Seymour, C. Jr., *Sculpture in Italy 1400 to 1500*, 1966, 134–8.

15. TRIUMPHAL ARCH OF KING ALFONSO OF ARAGON. Detail (photo: Anderson). A detail of the arch (pl. 14), showing sculpture on the inside left-hand portion of the arch, and revealing the combination of delicacy and boldness in the carving.

16. MAIN DOORWAY OF THE SALA DELLA IOLE. *Urbino, Palazzo Ducale* (photo: Alinari). The decorations of this room (see also pl. 17) are the richest in the Palace, but it is by no means clear who were the artists responsible. Over the doorway in the centre is carved one of the Duke's emblems, an exploding grenade.
Lit: Rotondi, *op. cit.* (text vol.) 137.

17. CHIMNEYPIECE IN THE SALA DELLA IOLE. *Urbino, Palazzo Ducale* (photo: Alinari). The shield displays the black eagle of Montefeltro. The caryatid figures supporting the chimneypiece are of Hercules and Iole (hence the room's name). The outstandingly beautiful friezes, the caryatids and shield figures, make up a chimneypiece of unprecedented importance. The likely artists are Michele di Giovanni, called il Greco, and his assistant Pasquino da Montepulciano.
Lit: Rotondi, *op. cit.*, 133–6.

18. A WINDOW. Attributed to Giovanni Antonio Amadeo, *c.* 1494–6. *Pavia, Certosa* (photo: Alinari).
Lit: Magenta, C., *La Certosa di Pavia*, 1897.

19. COURTYARD OF THE PALAZZO DUCALE. Attributed to Luciano Laurana. *Urbino* (photo: Anderson). Laurana is mentioned as Chief Architect at Urbino in a Ducal patent of 1468, but may have been working there earlier. He left Urbino in 1472. The many problems which arise in connexion with the Palace and the courtyard are dealt with extensively by Rotondi, *op. cit.* He emphasizes (pp. 219–23) the changing concept of the building from fortified castle into palace.

20. ESTIENNE CHEVALIER AND ST STEPHEN. By Jean Fouquet, *c.* 1450. Oil on panel, 93 × 85 cms. *Berlin-Dahlem, Gemäldegalerie* (museum photo). The other half of this exceptionally large diptych is in the Musée Royal at Antwerp; it is quite clear (*pace* Wescher, *loc. cit.*) that the whole was originally conceived as a diptych.
Lit: Wescher, P., *Jean Fouquet und seine Zeit*, 1945, 50 ff.; Sterling, C., Art Bull., XXVIII, 1946, 128.

21. CONRAD VON BUSNANG MONUMENT. By Nicolaus Gerhaerts von Leyden. Signed, 1464. *Strasbourg, Cathedral* (photo: Shricker).
Lit: Müller, T., *Sculpture of the 15th century in the Netherlands, Germany, France and Spain, 1400–1500*, 1966, 80.

22. TOMB OF MARTIN VAZQUEZ DE ARCE (and detail). Attributed to Sebastian de Almonacid. *Sigüenza, Cathedral* (photo: Mas). The subject died in 1486. The attribution of this tomb, and some others probably from the same workshop, is by no means certain.
Lit: Gomez-Moreno, M.E., *Breve Historia de la Escultura Española*, 1951, 63–4; Panofsky, E., *Tomb Sculpture*, 1964, 82.

23. LEONARDO BRUNI MONUMENT. By Bernardo Rossellino *c.* 1446–7. Marble. *Florence, S. Croce* (photo: Brogi). Bruni died in 1444, and the tomb was probably begun soon after his death; no documents of its commissioning appear to survive. The epitaph is by Carlo Marsuppini, Bruni's successor as Chancellor of the Florentine Republic.
Lit: Pope-Hennessy, 1958, 43, 297–8.

24. VIRGIN AND CHILD. By Antonio Rossellino, with assistant, 1461–65/6. Marble. *Florence, S. Miniato, Chapel of the Cardinal of Portugal* (photo: Brogi).
Lit: Hartt, F., Corti, G., Kennedy, C., *The Chapel of the Cardinal of Portugal 1434–1459*, 1964.

25. DOGE PIETRO MOCENIGO MONUMENT. Detail of the central portion. By Pietro Lombardo, with assistants, *c.* 1476–81. Istrian stone and marble. *Venice, SS Giovanni e Paolo* (photo: Böhm). Lombardo's assistants here are likely to have been his sons, of whom Tullio became the greatest sculptor of the family, a much more classicizing and 'learned' figure than his father.
Lit: Pope-Hennessy, 1958, 352.

26. HEAD OF A WARRIOR: THE DOGE ANDREA VENDRAMIN MONUMENT. By Tullio Lombardo, with assistants, 1492–*c.* 1495. Marble. *Venice, SS Giovanni e Paolo* (photo: Alinari). Originally in the Church of the Servi, the monument was moved to its present location in the nineteenth century and portions of it were dispersed; already recognized by Lombardo's contemporary, Sanudo, as a masterpiece. The illustration shows the head of a warrior standing left, flanking the monument.
Lit: Pope-Hennessy, 1958, 354–5.

27. TOMBSTONE OF LUDOVICO DIEDO. Niello. *Venice, SS Giovanni e Paolo* (photo: Cini).

28. POPE INNOCENT VIII MONUMENT. Detail. By Antonio del Pollaiuolo, 1492–8. Bronze. *Rome, St Peter's* (photo: Alinari). The Pope died in 1492, two months after receiving from the Sultan Bajazet the relic of the Holy Lance which he holds; Pope-Hennessy (*loc. cit.*) suggests that a wish to commemorate this fact perhaps accounted for the innovation of a life figure on the monument.
Lit: Pope-Hennessy, 1958, 318.

29. SIR JOHN HAWKWOOD. By Paolo Uccello. Signed, 1436. Fresco transferred to canvas, 820 × 515 cms. *Florence, Duomo* (photo: Soprintendenza alle Gallerie).
Lit: Pope-Hennessy, J., *Uccello*, 1950, 142.

30. DESIGN FOR A MONUMENT TO GIAN GALEAZZO SFORZA. By Filarete, 1460–65. Pen and ink. *Florence, Biblioteca Nazionale* (museum photo). An illustration to Filarete's *Trattato dell'Architettura*.

31. MAJOLICA DISH. By Jacopo Fattorini, 1514. 41·5 cms. *Cambridge, Fitzwilliam Museum* (photo: Fitzwilliam Museum, Cambridge). From the pottery at Cafaggiolo started by the Medici. Fattorini has been recognized as the author of several distinguished pieces; his style was much influenced by Botticelli.
Lit: Rackham, B., *Italian Maiolica*, 1952, 17.

32. THE TEMPIO MALATESTIANO (S. FRANCESCO). By Alberti. *Rimini* (photo: Gabinetto Fotografico Nazionale). The photograph shows the right-hand side of the church exterior, with the arcades holding sarcophagi; the façade was intended to have niches holding the sarcophagi of Sigismondo Malatesta and Isotta.
Lit: Ricci, C., *Il Tempio Malatestiano*, 1925.

33. PIAZZA PIO II. By Bernardo Rossellino, 1462–3. *Pienza* (photo: Kunsthistorisches Institut, Florence). The view is taken from the cortile of the Palazzo del Pretorio, and shows the Duomo, with the Palazzo Piccolomini at the right; the well-head before the Palace is, like the rest of the buildings, to the design of Rossellino.
Lit: Mannucci, G. B., *Pienza*, 1937; Schiavo, A., *Monumenti di Pienza*, 1942.

34. PLATINA BEFORE POPE SIXTUS IV. By Melozzo da Forlì, 1475–7. Fresco transferred to canvas (photo: Anderson). Painted for the Vatican Library.
Lit: Schmarsow, A., *Melozzo da Forlì*, 1886, 42–8; Buscaroli, R., *Melozzo da Forlì*, 1938, 52–6.

35. LUNA. By Agostino di Duccio (?), *c.* 1456. Marble relief. *Rimini, Tempio Malatestiano* (photo: Brogi). This is a pillar of the Holy Sacrament Chapel (or Chapel of the Planets), and typical of the delicately carved, proto-Botticelli style reliefs executed for the Tempio.
Lit: Pointner, A., *Die Werke des florentinischen Bildhauers Agostino d'Antonio di Duccio*, 1909, 83; Ricci, *op. cit.*, 455 ff; Mitchell, C., *Studi Romagnoli*, II, 1951, 77–90; Pope-Hennessy, 1958, 87–9; Seymour, *op. cit.*, 129–34.

36. GUARINO DA VERONA. By Matteo de' Pasti. Signed, *c.* 1446. Lead, 94 mm. *Washington, National Gallery of Art, Samuel H. Kress Collection* (museum photo). Probably executed when de' Pasti was engaged at the Court of Ferrara.
Lit: Hill, G. F., *A Corpus of Italian Medals of the Renaissance*, 1930, No. 158.

37. VITTORINO DA FELTRE. By Pisanello. Signed, 1446–7. Lead, 67 mm. (photo: Victoria & Albert Museum). See under pl. 38.

38. PELICAN IN ITS PIETY (reverse of medal pl. 37). Probably executed either just before or soon after Vittorino's death in 1446.
Lit: Hill, *op. cit.*, No. 38.

39. PIERO DE' MEDICI. By Mino da Fiesole. Signed, 1453. Marble. *Florence, Museo Nazionale* (photo: Alinari). The earliest surviving dated portrait bust from the Renaissance, and very early work by the sculptor; it was to be utilized by Bronzino for his portrait of the sitter. *London, National Gallery.*
Lit: Valentiner, W. R., *Studies of Italian Renaissance Sculpture*, 1950, 72–3.

40. SEA-MONSTER ABDUCTING A WOMAN. By Albrecht Dürer, *c.* 1498. Engraving 25·2 × 19 cms. *London, British Museum* (museum photo).
Lit: Panofsky, E., *The Life and Art of Albrecht Dürer*, 1955, 72–3.

41. NUDE YOUTH HOLDING A REARING HORSE. Studio of Filippo Lippi. Metal point on paper, heightened with white, 36 × 24·7 cms. *London, British Museum* (museum photo). Inspired by the statues of the Dioscuri at Rome.
Lit: Popham, A. E., and Pouncey, P., *Italian Drawings XIV–XV Centuries* (B.M. Cat.), 1950, No. 152.

42. APOLLO. By Antico, *c.* 1497. Bronze, 40 cms. *Venice, Ca' d'Oro* (photo: Rijksmuseum). A free reduction of the *Apollo Belvedere* by a sculptor working for the Gonzaga Court at Mantua, Pier Jacopo Alari Bonasolsi, who took 'Antico' as his nickname and produced several small bronze reproductions of classical antique sculpture.
Lit: *Italian Bronze Statuettes*, exhibition catalogue, Victoria and Albert Museum, 1961, No. 28.

43. INKWELL IN SHAPE OF A MONSTER. By Severo da Ravenna. Signed. Bronze, 11 × 25 cms. *New York, Blumka Collection* (photo: Blumka). The sculptor was active in Padua *c.* 1500.
Lit: Planiscig, L., *Jahrbuch der Kunsthistorischen Sammlungen in Wien*, 1935, 75 ff.; *Renaissance Bronzes in American Collections*, exhibition catalogue, Northampton, Mass., 1964, No. 8.

44. HERCULES AND ANTAEUS. By Antonio del Pollaiuolo. Bronze, 45 cms. *Florence, Museo Nazionale* (photo: Rijksmuseum). The first sculptural treatment in the Renaissance of a theme which was later to prove highly popular with sculptors.
Lit: Pope-Hennessy, 1958, 318.

45. A LAMP IN FORM OF AN ACROBAT. By Riccio. Bronze. *Paris, Bibliothèque Nationale* (photo: Giraudon). Variations of the design by Riccio exist; the present example is intended as a hanging lamp.
Lit: Planiscig, L., *Andrea Riccio*, 1927, 181–2.

46. SATYR AND SATYRESS. By Riccio. Bronze, 23·2 cms. *London, Victoria and Albert Museum* (photo: Rijksmuseum).
Lit: *Italian Bronze Statuettes*, exhibition cat., Victoria and Albert Museum, 1961, No. 55.

47. A MYTHOLOGICAL SUBJECT. Detail. By Piero di Cosimo. Panel, 65 × 183 cms. *London, National Gallery* (museum photo).
Lit: Davies, M., *The Earlier Italian Schools* (N.G. Cat.), 1961, 421–2.

48. VIEW OF VENICE. 1496. Wood inlay. *Venice, S. Marco* (photo: Cini). One of a series of similar scenes decorating cupboards in the Sacristy of S. Marco, signed as by '*Antonius et Paolus de Mantua . . .*' (restored in 1830).

49. ST AUGUSTINE IN HIS STUDY. Detail. By Vittore Carpaccio. Signed. *Venice, Scuola di S. Giorgio degli Schiavoni* (photo: Anderson).
Lit: Lauts, J., *Carpaccio*, 1962, 232–3.

50. MAJOLICA VASE. *c.* 1470–80. 37 cm. *London, Victoria and Albert Museum* (museum photo). From the factory at Faenza; the coat of arms has not been identified.
Lit: Rackham, *op. cit.*, 13–15.

51. NUPTIAL GOBLET. *c.* 1460–70. Glass. *Murano, Museo Vetrario* (photo: Böhm). Attributed to the Barovier family of glass-makers, and decorated with a Fountain of Love on a blue ground.
Lit: Mariacher, G., *Italian Blown Glass*, 1961, 25.

52. CASSONE WITH SOLOMON AND THE QUEEN OF SHEBA (?). Painted and gilded wood. Style of Francesco di Giorgio. *London, Victoria and Albert Museum* (museum photo).
Lit: Weller, A. Stuart, *Francesco di Giorgio, 1439–1501*, 1943, 298.

53. RELIQUARY OF CHARLES THE BOLD. By Gérard Loyet, *c.* 1467. Gold and enamel, height 53 cms. *Liége, Cathedral* (photo: copyright A.C.L.). Charles succeeded his father as Duke of Burgundy in 1467 and presented the reliquary to the Cathedral in 1471. The Saint is St George. This is one of the very few surviving gold pieces of the type often commissioned by the Dukes of Burgundy, and one of the most splendid.
Lit: *Flanders in the Fifteenth Century*, exhibition cat., Detroit, 1960, 298–300.

54. THE EXECUTION OF ST JOHN THE BAPTIST. After Antonio del Pollaiuolo. Embroidery, 22 × 30 cms. *Florence, Museo dell' Opera del Duomo* (photo: Alinari). One of a series of embroideries for vestments, all dealing with the story of St John the Baptist. Commissioned in 1466, the designs were finally paid for in 1480.
Lit: Cruttwell, M., *Antonio Pollaiuolo*, 1907, 100–115 (probably still the clearest account).

55. THE MONTH OF APRIL. Detail. By Cossa, 1469–70. Fresco. *Ferrara, Palazzo Schifanoia* (photo: Villani).
Lit: Neppi, A., *Francesco del Cossa*, 1958, 11 ff.

56. THE LOGGIA DEL CONSIGLIO. Associated doubtfully with Fra Giocondo. *Verona* (photo: Quiresi).
Lit: Brenzoni, R., in *Atti dell' Accademia di Arte, Scienza e Letteratura di Verona*, 1958; the same author in *L'Arena*, 12 January 1960.

57. A CONCERT. By Lorenzo Costa. Panel, 95 × 75 cms. *London, National Gallery* (museum photo).
Lit: Gould, C., *The Sixteenth-Century Italian Schools (excluding the Venetian)* (N.G. Cat.), 1962, 44–5.

58. THE PIETÀ. By Botticelli. Panel, 140 × 207 cms. *Munich, Alte Pinakothek* (photo: National Gallery, London). Sometimes unreasonably doubted, the picture is certainly a fine autograph work. It is often called late work, but this is not necessarily so. The beardless Christ seems derived from an antique sarcophagus figure – probably a Meleager. In this connection it is worth recalling that Alberti, in *De Pittura*, speaks of having seen in Rome an *istoria* (probably a sarcophagus relief) of Meleager, in which the lifeless quality of the corpse was particularly remarkable. Christ's unwounded body is a hint towards the concept of Michelangelo's *Pietà* (pl. 109).

59. THE CORONATION OF THE VIRGIN. By Giovanni Bellini. Signed, *c.* 1475–80. Oil on panel, 262 × 240 cms. *Pesaro, Museo Civico* (museum photo). Central portion of a polyptych which survives intact in its original frame, except for the *Pietà* now in the Vatican Museum. The picture's date has been much discussed, but further evidence for the date given here is provided by Fahy, *loc. cit.*

Lit: Robertson, G., 'The Earlier Work of Giovanni Bellini,' J.W.C.I., XXIII, 1960, 45–59; Fahy, E. P., Jr, Art Bull., 1964, 216–18.

60. PALAZZO CORNER-SPINELLI. Attributed to Mauro Coducci. *Venice* (photo: Alinari). Sometimes attributed to Pietro Lombardo, but a majority of scholars favour the attribution to Coducci.
Lit: Angelini, *op. cit.*, 82–5.

61. PALAZZO RUCELLAI. By Alberti, 1446–51. Executed by Bernardo Rossellino. *Florence* (photo: Bazzechi).

62. LUCA PACIOLI AND A PUPIL. By 'Jaco. Bar.'. Signed, 1495. Wood, 99 × 120 cms. *Naples, Museo di Capodimonte* (photo: Alinari). Pacioli (1450 – after 1510) is portrayed teaching by an unknown painter who signs as above; that this signature stands for Jacopo de' Barbari is no longer an accepted hypothesis.

63. VITRUVIAN MAN. By Francesco di Giorgio. Pen and ink on parchment. *Florence, Biblioteca Laurenziana.* (Cod. Ashburnham 361) (museum photo).
Lit: Weller, *op. cit.*, 273–5.

64. VITRUVIAN MAN. By Leonardo da Vinci, *c.* 1485–90. Pen and ink on paper, 34·3 × 24·5 cms. *Venice, Accademia* (photo: Alinari).
Lit: Popham, A. E., *The Drawings of Leonardo da Vinci*, 1947, No. 215.

65. S. MARIA DELLE CARCERI (exterior). By Giuliano da Sangallo, begun 1484. *Prato* (photo: Quiresi).
Lit: Clausse, G., *Les San Gallo*, 1900, I, 84–105; Marchini, G., *Giuliano da Sangallo*, 1942, 87.

66. S. MARIA DELLE CARCERI (interior) (photo: Alinari).
See under pl. 65.

67. GARDEN OF LOVE. Attributed to the school of Antonio Vivarini. Panel, 159 × 241 cms. *Melbourne, National Gallery of Victoria* (museum photo).
Lit: Hoff, U., *Catalogue of European Paintings before Eighteen Hundred*, 1961, 135–7.

68. AN IDEAL TOWNSCAPE. Circle of Piero della Francesca. Panel, 200 × 60 cms. *Urbino, Palazzo Ducale* (photo: Soprintendenza alle Gallerie). The authorship of this fine painting is not certain, but several critics incline to accept it as by Piero della Francesca himself. The suggestion that this picture and a comparable, but less distinguished, panel at Baltimore represent respectively the Comic and Tragic stage as described by Vitruvius originates with Krautheimer, *loc. cit.*
Lit: Krautheimer, R., in *Gazette des Beaux-Arts*, Jan.–June 1948, 327ff; *Mostra di Quattro Maestri del Primo Rinascimento*, Florence, 1954, 128–9.

69. THE FLAGELLATION OF CHRIST. By Piero della Francesca. Signed. Panel, 59 × 81·5 cms. *Urbino, Palazzo Ducale* (photo: Soprintendenza alle Gallerie).
Lit: Wittkower, R. and Carter, B. A. R., 'The Perspective of Piero della Francesca's Flagellation', J.W.C.I., XVI, 1953, 292ff; *Mostra di Quattro Maestri del Primo Rinascimento*, Florence, 1954, No. 41.

70. THE FLAGELLATION. Detail of pl. 69.

71. THE TRINITY. By Masaccio, *c.* 1426–7. Fresco, 489 × 317 cms. *Florence, S. Maria Novella* (photo: Soprintendenza alle Gallerie). Cross-section demonstration of the composition and reference to the ideas of Cardinal Nicholas of Cusa in connexion with the use of mathematics are provided by Berti, *loc. cit.* The pre-Vasari sources mention the skeleton below the main scene which has only comparatively recently been recovered.
Lit: Berti, L., *Masaccio*, 1964, 110–18.

72. SEVEN SACRAMENTS TRIPTYCH (central panel). By Rogier van der Weyden, *c.* 1453. Oil on panel, 200×97 cms. *Antwerp, Musée Royal des Beaux-Arts* (photo: copyright A.C.L.). The central panel is usually accepted as autograph work; the side panels (see pl. 73), showing the Sacraments, as of lower quality and of studio execution. The triptych was commissioned by Jean Chevrot, Bishop of Tournai, and its iconography is unique.
Lit: Panofsky, E., *Early Netherlandish Painting*, 1953, I, 282–5.

73. BOYS AFTER CONFIRMATION. Studio of Rogier van der Weyden. Detail of the left-hand panel of the Seven Sacraments Triptych (see pl. 72).

74. ANNUNCIATION TABERNACLE. Detail. By Donatello, *c.* 1428–33. Limestone, partly coloured. *Florence, S. Croce* (photo: Alinari).
Lit: Janson, H. W., *The Sculpture of Donatello*, 1957, II, 103–8; Pope-Hennessy, 1958, 276–7.

75. THE ANNUNCIATION. By Benedetto da Maiano, 1489. Marble. *Naples, S. Anna dei Lombardi* (photo: Anderson). The central portion of the marble altar in the Mastrogiudici Chapel of S. Anna dei Lombardi, the church where the upper portion of the tomb of Maria of Aragon (1481) is by the same sculptor.
Lit: Dussler, L., *Benedetto da Majano*, 1924, 39–42; Pope-Hennessy, 1958, 308.

76. S. SPIRITO (interior). By Brunelleschi. Begun 1436. *Florence* (photo: Paolo Monti).
Lit: Luporini, E., *Brunelleschi, Forma e Ragione*, 1964, 82–132.

77. THE ANNUNCIATION. Detail. By the Master of the Aix Annunciation, 1442–5. Oil on panel, 155×175 cms. *Aix-en-Provence, Church of the Madeleine* (photo: Bulloz). The central panel of an altarpiece (the wings now at Rotterdam and Brussels) by an unknown, presumably French, painter. Commissioned by the draper Pierre Corpici for an altar in the Cathedral of Saint-Sauveur at Aix.
Lit: Boyer, J., *Gazette des Beaux-Arts*, Dec. 1959, 301–11; *ibid.*, Sept. 1960, 137–144.

78. THE ANNUNCIATION. By Konrad Witz, *c.* 1444. Panel, 158 × 120·5 cms. *Nuremburg, Germanisches Nationalmuseum* (museum photo).
Lit: Gantner, J., *Konrad Witz*, 1943, 31.

79. THE MIRACULOUS DRAUGHT OF FISHES. By Konrad Witz. Signed, 1444. Oil on panel, 132 × 154 cms. *Geneva, Musée d'Art et d'Histoire* (photo: Arland). Painted for the Cathedral of Saint-Pierre at Geneva.
Lit: Gantner, *op. cit.*, 29–30.

80. THE DEATH OF ST FRANCIS. By Domenico Ghirlandaio, 1485. Fresco. *Florence, S. Trinita* (photo: Soprintendenza alle Gallerie). One of the frescoes of the Saint's life painted for the chapel built by Francesco Sassetti, completed at the same date as Ghirlandaio's altarpiece (pl. 81).

81. THE ADORATION OF THE SHEPHERDS. By Domenico Ghirlandaio, 1485. Oil on panel, 167×167 cms. *Florence, S. Trinita* (photo: Anderson). The altarpiece in the Sassetti Chapel; the use of antique classical motifs there is extended to the black marble sarcophagi, in Roman style, which contain the bodies of Sassetti and his wife.

82. A TRIPLE-HEADED HERM. 1467 (?). Woodcut. *London, National Gallery Library* (museum photo). From Francesco Colonna's *Hypnerotomachia Poliphili*, published in 1499 at Venice by the famous publisher Aldus Manutius.

Lit: Casella, M. T., and Pozzi, G., *Francesco Colonna, Biografia e Opere*, 1959, II, 150 ff. (discussion of the illustrations).

83. EQUESTRIAN MONUMENT OF GATTAMELATA. By Donatello, *c.* 1450. Bronze, *c.* 340 cms. *Padua, Piazza del Santo* (photo: Anderson). The *condottiere* Erasmo da Narni, nicknamed Gattamelata, died at Padua early in 1443 and later the same year Donatello arrived there. It was probably not at first intended to produce a bronze statue in antique style but a stone one, set into a wall. Donatello's final result, set up in 1453, was to give – in a way unparalleled before – antique imperial trappings to a modern soldier.
Lit: Janson, *op. cit.*, II, 151–61; Pope-Hennessy, 1958, 283–4.

84. ST JAMES ON HIS WAY TO MARTYRDOM. By Andrea Mantegna, *c.* 1450. Fresco. *Padua, Eremitani* (destroyed). Photo: Anderson. One of the fresco cycle in the Cappella Ovetari dealing with the life of St James the Greater to whom – together with St Christopher – the church is dedicated. The chapel was bombed in 1944, during the Second World War; some frescoes were lost entirely, others survive in fragments, and two previously transferred to canvas escaped damage.
Lit: *Andrea Mantegna*, exhibition cat., Mantua, 1961, 9–13.

85. 'CUPID-ATYS.' By Donatello, *c.* 1440. Bronze, 104 cms. *Florence, Museo Nazionale* (photo: Brogi). First mentioned by Vasari and called 'Mercury', in 1568. Nothing is known of its commissioner or the circumstances of its commission. When mentioned by Vasari it belonged to Giovanni, son of Agnolo Doni. The 'Cupid-Atys' title is here retained for convenience, but is almost certainly wrong. It is likely that the statue combines attributes of several kinds and hence Vasari's difficulty in correctly identifying it. Panofsky, *loc. cit.*, sees it as 'Time as a Playful Child' and suggests the object held up may have been a dice. Is it possible it was a butterfly (for Psyche) and that it is really a Cupid? Possibly of significance is the fact that so many attributes (poppies on the belt, faun's tail, etc.) are not visible when the statue is seen from the front.
Lit: Janson, *op. cit.*, II, 143–7; Panofsky, E., *Renaissance and Renascences in Western Art*, 1965 ed., 169.

86. BOY WITH BAGPIPES. By Andrea della Robbia. Terracotta, 45·4 cms. *London, Victoria and Albert Museum* (museum photo).
Lit: Pope-Hennessy, J., *Catalogue of the Italian Sculpture in the Victoria and Albert Museum*, 1964, I, 215–16.

87. PUTTO HOLDING A DOLPHIN. By Andrea Verrocchio, *c.* 1470. Bronze, 69 cms. *Florence, Museo Nazionale* (photo: Alinari). Executed probably for Piero de' Medici ('il Gottoso') who died in 1469, or (as Vasari says) for Lorenzo the Magnificent, for the villa at Careggi, and serving there as a fountain figure. Moved later to the Palazzo Vecchio cortile where it is now replaced by a copy.
Lit: Planiscig, L., *Andrea del Verrocchio*, 1941, 52; Pope-Hennessy, 1958, 312.

88. THE RAPE OF HELEN. By a Follower of Fra Angelico, *c.* 1450. Panel, 51 × 61 cms. *London, National Gallery* (museum photo). Presumed to be part of the decoration originally of a chest.
Lit: Davies, M., *The Earlier Italian Schools* (N.G. Cat.), 1961, 33–4.

89. ARISTOTLE AND PHYLLIS. By the Master of the Housebook. Drypoint. *Oxford, Ashmolean Museum* (photo: by courtesy of the Museum).
Lit: Stange, A., *Der Hausbuchmeister*, 1958, 38 (No. 57).

90. THE BOYHOOD OF CICERO. By Vincenzo Foppa. Fresco, 96 × 132 cms.

London, Wallace Collection (photo: Crown Copyright). The fresco for long passed as merely of a boy reading Cicero, until correctly identified by Waterhouse.

Lit: Waterhouse, E. K., *Burl. Mag.*, XCII, 1950, 177.

91. THE MARTELLI MIRROR. Bronze, 22·9 cms. *London, Victoria and Albert Museum* (museum photo).

Lit: Pope-Hennessy, J., *Catalogue of the Italian Sculpture in the Victoria and Albert Museum*, 1964, I, 325–9.

92. HOLYWATER STOUP. By Antonio Federighi, c. 1462–3. Marble. *Siena, Cathedral* (photo: Alinari).

Lit: Schmarsow, A., 'Antonio Federighi de' Tolomei', *Repertorium für Kunstwissenschaft*, XII, 1889, 284–5.

93. PAN. By Luca Signorelli. Signed. Canvas, 194 × 257 cms. *Berlin, Kaiser-Friedrich-Museum* (destroyed) (museum photo). Usually identified with 'some naked gods' painted on canvas for Lorenzo de' Medici, according to Vasari (who as a boy knew Signorelli). The exact significance of the scene has been much discussed without any fully acceptable explanation being so far proposed.

94. EVE. By Antonio Rizzo. Signed. Marble, 204 cms. *Venice, Palazzo Ducale* (photo: Anderson).

Lit: Pope-Hennessy, 1958, 349–50.

95. PALLAS AND A CENTAUR. By Botticelli. Canvas, 207 × 148 cms. *Florence, Uffizi* (photo: Soprintendenza alle Gallerie).

Lit: Gombrich, E. H., 'Botticelli's Mythologies', *J.W.C.I.*, VIII, 1945, 50–53.

96. THE VIRGIN OF THE ROCKS. By Leonardo da Vinci, c. 1483. Canvas, 199 × 122 cms. *Paris, Musée du Louvre* (museum photo).

97. MONA LISA. By Leonardo da Vinci. Panel, 77 × 53 cms. *Paris, Musée du Louvre* (photo: Agraci).

98. PULPIT-BEARER. By Anton Pilgram, c. 1485–90. Sandstone, 115 cms. *East-Berlin, Staatliche Museen* (museum photo).

Lit: *Deutsche Bildwerke aus sieben Jahrhunderten* (museum cat.), 1958, 42–3.

99. TOMBSTONE OF BISHOP DONATO MEDICI. Detail. By Antonio Rossellino (?), 1475. Stone. *Pistoia, Cathedral* (photo: Alinari).

Lit: Gottschalk, H., *Antonio Rossellino*, 1930, 187.

100. BUST OF A WOMAN (MARIETTA STROZZI?). By Antonio Rossellino. Marble, 52.5 cms. *Berlin-Dahlem, Staatliche Museen* (museum photo). The identification with Marietta Strozzi is far from sure and depends on the association made by Bode with a bust of her executed by Desiderio da Settignano. Pope-Hennessy shows that Rossellino is the likely sculptor.

Lit: Pope-Hennessy, 1958, 301 and 304.

101. SELF-PORTRAIT. By Albrecht Dürer. Signed, 1498. Oil on panel, 52 × 41 cms. *Madrid, Museo del Prado* (museum photo).

Lit: Panofsky, E., *The Life and Art of Albrecht Dürer*, 1955 ed., 42–3.

102. PEASANTS GOING TO MARKET. By Martin Schongauer. Signed. Engraving, 16·3 × 16·3 cms. *London, British Museum* (museum photo).

Lit: Baum, J., *Martin Schongauer*, 1948, 36.

103. THE NATIVITY AT NIGHT. Attributed to Geertgen tot Sint Jans. Panel, 34 × 25 cms. *London, National Gallery* (museum photo). An early but not the earliest treatment of the subject at night in non-Italian painting.

Lit: Davies, M., *Early Netherlandish School* (N.G. Cat.), 1955, 43.

104. 'CUER' AND HIS COMPANIONS FIND 'AMITTIE' AND 'COMPAGNIE' FISHING.

Vienna, Staatsbibliotek (museum photo). From *Le Livre du Cuer d'Amours Espris* executed for King René of Anjou (1409–80), by an unknown painter, to illustrate the King's allegorical prose-cum-poem work.

Lit: Smital, O., and Winkler, E., *René Duc d'Anjou: Livre du Cuer d'Amours Espris*, 1927.

105. THE GARDEN OF DELIGHTS. Detail. By Hieronymus Bosch. Oil on panel, total area 220 × 195 cms. *Madrid, Museo del Prado* (museum photo).

Lit: Tolnay, C. de, *Hieronymus Bosch*, 1966, 360–63.

106. BATTLE OF SEA-MONSTERS. By Andrea Mantegna. Engraving, 33 × 44·7 cms. *London, British Museum* (museum photo). The right-hand portion of two engravings of the same theme by Mantegna.

Lit: Hind, A. H., *Early Italian Engraving*, v, 1948, 15–16.

107. CHRIST GIVING THE KEYS TO ST PETER. By Pietro Perugino, 1481–2. Fresco. *Vatican, Sistine Chapel* (photo: Biblioteca Hertziana). For the significance of this scene in the series from the lives of Christ and Moses frescoed for Sixtus IV, see Ettlinger, *loc. cit.*

Lit: Ettlinger, L. D., *The Sistine Chapel before Michelangelo*, 1965, 90–93.

108. THE BETROTHAL OF THE VIRGIN. By Raphael. Signed, 1504. Panel, 170 × 117 cms. *Milan, Brera* (photo: Anderson). The composition is based on Perugino's of the same subject (at Caen); a comparison between the two is made by Wölfflin, *Classic Art*, 1952 ed., 77–9.

Lit: Camesasca, E., *Tutta la Pittura di Raffaello* (*i Quadri*), 1962, 37.

109. PIETÀ. By Michelangelo. Signed. Completed probably *c.* 1499–1500. Marble, 174 cms. *Rome, St Peter's* (photo: Alinari). A tendency to regard the Madonna's left hand as wrongly restored in the eighteenth century is corrected by Lavin, *loc. cit.*, after recent careful examination.

Lit: Tolnay, C. de, *The Youth of Michelangelo*, 1947, 145–50; Pope-Hennessy, J., *Italian High Renaissance and Baroque Sculpture*, cat. vol., 1963, 5–6; Lavin, I., Art Bull., March 1966, 103–4.

110. THE S. GIOBBE ALTARPIECE. By Giovanni Bellini. Signed. Panel, 471 × 258 cms. *Venice, Accademia* (photo: Cini). The exact date of this key altarpiece is not clear, but there are good grounds for thinking it cannot be later than *c.* 1487–9 and not earlier than 1476.

Lit: Moschini Marconi, S., *Opere d'Arte dei Secoli XIV e XV* (Accademia cat.), 1955, 67–9.

111. SS. FRANCIS, JOHN THE BAPTIST AND JOB (detail of 110).

The publishers and author express grateful thanks to all those who have kindly permitted the illustration here of works in their care or possession.

Books for Further Reading

It should be noted that books, not articles, are the subject of this list, which is further restricted as far as possible to works available in English.

The subject of the Renaissance, even when interpreted entirely in connexion with art, is too vast for a full bibliography to be attempted here. In conjunction with the selection of books mentioned below, the reader is advised to glance at the bibliographies provided by two companion volumes in the present series, *Gothic* by George Henderson and *Mannerism* by John Shearman, both published in 1967.

Nothing probably will ever replace Jacob Burckhardt's *Die Cultur der Renaissance in Italien* (first published 1860) of which there is a convenient illustrated English edition published by the Phaidon Press, 1945. The first French edition of Burckhardt, of 1958, is richly and intelligently illustrated. An invaluable recent supplement, in effect, to Burckhardt is provided by the group of six essays in *The Renaissance: a reconsideration of the theories and interpretations of the age*, T. Helton (ed.), 1964, each of which has its own bibliography. For the whole problem of Renaissance style, and for much else, see E. Panofsky, *Renaissance and Renascences in Western Art*, 1965 (second edition). Pater's *The Renaissance* (first published 1873) does in an obviously limited way continue to do what its author claimed: 'touch what I think the chief points in that complex, many-sided movement'. It is a book attractive for being more profound than it seems – unlike much modern scholarship.

Although history is not dealt with fully here, it is worth looking at H. Baron, *The Crisis of the Early Italian Renaissance*, 1955, and N. Rubinstein, *The Government of Florence under the Medici 1434 to 1494*, 1966. A useful grasp on the wide field indicated by its title is provided by P. Laven, *Renaissance Italy 1464–1534*, 1966 (with good bibliography). Stimulating and brilliant is F. Chabod's *Machiavelli and the Italian Renaissance*, 1958; also worth reading is D. Hay, *The Italian Renaissance in its Historical Background*, 1961. Many valuable studies on topics not commonly discussed (e.g. 'War and Public Opinion' and 'Latin Verse of the High Renaissance') in *Italian Renaissance Studies*, E. F. Jacob (ed.), 1960. For the whole European scene, too rarely treated in this way: D. Hay, *The Renaissance*, 1963; W. K. Ferguson, *The Renaissance*, 1964; and Myron P. Gilmore *The World of Humanism, 1453–1517*, 1962, containing a remarkable bibliography (up to 1958) of nearly fifty pages, covering all aspects of the period. The same author's *Humanists and Jurists: Six Studies in the Renaissance*, 1963, also ranges over Europe. The catalogue of the exhibition at Brussels, *L'Europe Humaniste*, 1954, and the commemorative volume by A. Chastel, *The Age of Humanism*, 1963, are useful. A distinguished symposium (with essays by, among others, Panofsky, Ferguson, and R. S. Lopez), *The Renaissance*, 1962, manages to deal with many aspects of the age, from economics to art. More specialized and partly invalidated is A. von Martin, *Sociology of the Renaissance* (Harper Torch-book, edition), 1963. Interesting as a guide to the business environment and attitudes of people like the Arnolfini is R. de Roover, *Money, Banking and Credit in Medieval Bruges*, 1948. Strictly concerned with the sixteenth century but interesting also for comment on earlier periods is H. Osborn Taylor, *The French Mind*, 1962.

Changing concepts of the Renaissance across the centuries are fascinatingly discussed by W. K. Ferguson, *The Renaissance in Historical Thought*, 1948; and the same author's collected papers, *Renaissance Studies*, 1963, touch on many interesting points. Those interested in the history of history will also enjoy *England and the Italian Renaissance*, 1963 (revised edition), by J. R. Hale, who is also the author of a Time-Life publication, *Renaissance*, 1965.

On the humanist and philosophical background: F. Seebohm, *The Oxford Reformers* (first published 1867; abridged Everyman edition, 1929); W. H. Woodward, *Vittorino da Feltre and other Humanist Educators*, 1897, still impressively good; R. Weiss, *Humanism in England during the Fifteenth Century*, 1941; P. O. Kristeller, *The Classics and Renaissance Thought*, 1955; E. Cassirer, *The Individual and the Cosmos in Renaissance Philosophy*, 1963 (considerable discussion of Nicholas of Cusa); *The Renaissance Philosophy of Man*, E. Cassirer and P. O. Kristeller (eds.), 1963 (translations of important passages from Renaissance philosophers, with individual introductions).

On music: P. H. Lang, *Music in Western Civilization*, 1941; G. Reese, *Music in the Renaissance*, 1959; volume 2 of *A History of Music*, A. Robertson and D. Stevens (eds.), 1965 edition.

On particular aspects of the arts in relation to the period: A. Warburg *Gesammelte Schriften*, 2 vols, 1932 (containing several still very relevant studies, e.g. on Ghirlandaio and the Sassetti); M. Wackernagel, *Der Lebensraum des Künstlers in der florentinischen Renaissance*, 1938; A. Chastel, *Marsile Ficin et l'Art*, 1954; *Juste de Gand, Berruguete et la Cour d'Urbino*, exhibition at Ghent, 1957; F. Saxl, *Lecturès*, 2 vols, 1957 (several directly relevant studies, e.g. 'Jacopo Bellini and Mantegna as antiquarians', and much that generally illuminates the Renaissance); E. Wind, *Pagan Mysteries in the Renaissance*, 1958; *Decorative Arts of the Italian Renaissance 1400–1600*, exhibition at Detroit, 1958–9; *Flanders in the Fifteenth Century*, exhibition at Detroit, 1960; A. Chastel, *Art et Humanisme à Florence au temps de Laurent le Magnifique*, 1961 (includes wider studies than the title suggests, e.g. on Courts of Rimini and Urbino); R. Wittkower, *Architectural Principles in the Age of Humanism*, 1962, revised edition; A. Blunt, *Artistic Theory in Italy 1450–1600*, 1962 edition; O. Benesch, *The Art of the Renaissance in Northern Europe*, 1965, revised and very well illustrated edition; W. Stechow, *Northern Renaissance Art 1400–1600* (Sources and Documents series), 1966; E. H. Gombrich, *Norm and Form*, 1966 (first volume of the author's collected Renaissance studies, of which the second is forthcoming); A. R. Turner, *The Vision of Landscape in Renaissance Italy*, 1966; J. Pope-Hennessy, *The Portrait in the Renaissance*, 1967.

Finally, a few further books which might be missed and which I have found valuable and thought-provoking: D. Cameron Allen, *The Legend of Noah*, 1949; H. Haydn, *The Counter-Renaissance*, 1950; also useful, M. Whitcomb, *A Literary Sourcebook of the Renaissance*, 1903.

Index